Social Issues
in Literature

Male and Female Roles in Ernest Hemingway's *The Sun Also Rises*

Other Books in the Social Issues in Literature Series:

Social Issues
in Literature

Male and Female Roles in Ernest Hemingway's *The Sun Also Rises*

Dedria Bryfonski, Book Editor

GREENHAVEN PRESS
A part of Gale, Cengage Learning

GALE
CENGAGE Learning™

Detroit • New York • San Francisco • New Haven, Conn • Waterville, Maine • London

Christine Nasso, *Publisher*
Elizabeth Des Chenes, *Managing Editor*

© 2008 Greenhaven Press, a part of Gale, Cengage Learning

Gale and Greenhaven Press are registered trademarks used herein under license.

For more information, contact:
Greenhaven Press
27500 Drake Rd.
Farmington Hills, MI 48331-3535
Or you can visit our Internet site at gale.cengage.com

For product information and technology assistance, contact us at

Gale Customer Support, 1-800-877-4253
For permission to use material from this text or product, submit all requests online at
www.cengage.com/permissions

Further permissions questions can be emailed to permissionrequest@cengage.com

Articles in Greenhaven Press anthologies are often edited for length to meet page requirements. In addition, original titles of these works are changed to clearly present the main thesis and to explicitly indicate the author's opinion. Every effort is made to ensure that Greenhaven Press accurately reflects the original intent of the authors. Every effort has been made to trace the owners of copyrighted material.

Cover image © Richard Melloul/Sygma/Corbis.

ISBN-13: 978-0-7377-4020-2

Library of Congress Control Number: 2008923211

Printed in the United States of America
1 2 3 4 5 6 7 12 11 10 09 08

Contents

Chapter 1: Background on Ernest Hemingway

Chapter 2: *The Sun Also Rises* and Male and Female Roles

Chapter 3: Contemporary Perspectives on Male and Female Roles

Introduction

In comparing early commentary on Ernest Hemingway and his first novel, *The Sun Also Rises*, with later analyses, the contemporary reader may have the sense of reading about two different writers and two different books. The understanding of Hemingway—and thus the appreciation for many of his works—underwent a sea change in the late 1970s as more biographical information about him became available. It began when his older sister, Marcelline Hemingway Sanford, wrote a memoir titled *At the Hemingways: A Family Portrait* in 1961. In 1976, his fourth wife, Mary, published *How It Was*. Both books revealed some unusual aspects of his upbringing and marital relations that departed from the standard bounds of masculinity and heterosexuality. But the greatest change in the perception of Hemingway came as his papers and manuscripts became available to scholars through the Hemingway Collection at the John Fitzgerald Kennedy Library in Boston. Mary Hemingway began depositing these papers as early as 1972, and the collection was officially opened in 1980. These materials, and in particular the unfinished novel *The Garden of Eden*, revealed a writer concerned with themes of androgyny, homosexuality, cross-dressing, sex role reversals, and transsexuality. Rereading Hemingway's fiction in light of these revelations, critics began to recognize that, far from the persona Hemingway had projected of the macho writer at home in a man's world, he actually had a complex view of human relationships and gender. As a result, Hemingway's life and fiction underwent one of the most extensive reassessments in literary scholarship.

To understand the impact of Hemingway's experiences and cultural milieu on his writing, it's important to recognize the extent to which the author used his own experiences in his writing. Shortly after Hemingway's death, the novelist Nelson Algren made the distinction "between a man who represents his time, like John Dos Passos, and one who, like Hemingway, made his time represent him." Unlike earlier writers like Henry James who were observers of life, Hemingway was an active participant in life's more adventurous aspects. The source for his fiction was his own life; therefore, he lived life at full tilt, trying to see and experience as much as possible. The characters and many events in *The Sun Also Rises* are drawn from a trip Hemingway and his first wife, Hadley, made to the Fiesta of San Fermin to see the bullfights in Pamplona, Spain, in the summer of 1925. They were accompanied by novelist Harold Loeb, English socialite Lady Duff Twysden, her fiancé Pat Guthrie, and Hemingway's fishing friend Bill Smith. These individuals are generally believed to be models for the characters Robert Cohn, Lady Brett Ashley, Mike Campbell, and Bill Gorton, respectively. Hemingway began writing the novel following the trip and finished the first draft only two months later in September.

Hemingway borrowed from life not only for plot and characters, but also for the themes of his works. Hemingway lived an unconventional life, far different from the lives of mainstream Americans. His early upbringing, the experiences of being an expatriate in Paris during the 1920s, the Jazz Age, the personalities of the four women he chose as wives—all of these contributed to Hemingway's sophisticated awareness of the impact that cultural and historical forces have on personal relationships and the pressures they bring to bear on issues of gender. Thus, the Hemingway concerned with male bonding, drinking, and masculine pursuits of bullfighting, fishing, and safaris—as he was depicted in early criticism—morphs into the author concerned with cultural perceptions of gender in criticism post-1980. Although the plots of his novels may center on macho sports, their themes are love and relationships and what it means to be heroic in a nihilistic world.

The Jazz Age was born at the end of World War I. Cultural historian Sandra Gilbert argues that World War I had very different effects on men than it did on women: "As young men became increasingly alienated from their prewar selves, women seemed to become, as if by some uncanny swing of history's pendulum, even more powerful." When the men went off to war, a vacuum was created. Into this vacuum, women redefined their roles—they went to work, and shortly after the end of the war, received the right to vote in the United States. Thus, Gilbert concludes, "the war that has traditionally been defined as an apocalypse of masculinism seems to have led to an apotheosis of femaleness."

World War I was "The Great War" and "The War to End All Wars"—a conflict so bloody and destructive and affecting so much of the western world that it disrupted society as no war or battle had done before. Coming home from the war, men had lost their innocence. Their perspectives had broadened. They became more contemplative while at the same time being more open to new experiences. At the same time, the women who had been left behind had also changed profoundly. For the first time, many of these women left their homes and entered the workforce. In this working environment, they became more independent, forming relationships outside the family circle. They also adopted more comfortable, less constricting styles of dress. Many also took up smoking and drinking. In these pursuits, they were greatly influenced by the popularization in cinema and fiction of the flapper. The term "flapper" referred to the floppy rain boots worn by young, liberated ladies in England. The flapper wore makeup, a bobbed hairstyle, and short skirts that displayed silk stockings. The ideal flapper had a thin and boyish figure; those not blessed by nature with a boyish shape often taped down their breasts to create that effect. The flapper smoked, drank liquor, danced, and enjoyed a variety of partners. While relatively few working women of the 1920s were flappers, more modest versions of flapper behavior and clothing caught on with a wide variety of women. The androgynous clothing styles of designers such as Coco Chanel redefined female sexuality and served to blur the lines between men's and women's roles in society.

At that time Hemingway was part of a literary coterie led by Gertrude Stein in Paris, where some women went beyond flapper fashion to dress in a frankly mannish manner. As Virginia Woolf would later say, "We are what we wear, and therefore, since we can wear anything, we can be anyone." Hemingway, writing *The Sun Also Rises* in the early 1920s, was writing in a time when the New Woman of the Jazz Age was coming into her own. This New Woman had a stronger masculine side, based on her need to become more independent. At the same time, men returning from the war had been sensitized by their experiences. Thus the Jazz Age was a time of the destabilization of gender roles.

To the gender fluidity resulting from World War I, Hemingway brought his own early experiences with gender reversal. His sister Marcelline wrote in *At the Hemingways* that their mother, Grace, treated Ernest as Marcelline's female twin, dressing him in girl's clothes into their early school years. Throughout most of Hemingway's life, his father struggled with depression and mental problems. As a result of this, his mother assumed responsibility for the family and took on the traditionally male role. Hemingway, perhaps fearing the often hereditary nature of depression and nervous disorders, blamed his mother for destroying his father and their happy family unit. Later in life, he would call her "the all-time, All-American bitch." Hemingway's son Gregory would later say he was forbidden by his father to visit his grandmother because "she was androgynous"—a description presumably based on Grace's friendship with Ruth Arnold, her voice student who lived with the family.

Throughout his life, Hemingway would be drawn to women who were older, richer, and professionally accomplished. His first recorded love, nurse Agnes von Kurowsky, was seven years his senior. His first wife, Hadley, was six years older than Hemingway and her trust fund was an important means of support during the early years of their marriage. His second wife, Pauline, came from an extremely wealthy family. To marry her, he converted to Catholicism. Her family money, rather than earnings from his writings, supported them through most of their marriage. Perhaps his most challenging wife was Martha Gellhorn, an accomplished writer and correspondent in her own right. During World War II, Hemingway found himself competing with his wife as a war correspondent. His fourth and final wife, Mary Welsh, was also a writer. In 1976, she published *How It Was* in which she revealed that—just as the androgynous couple did in the posthumously published *The Garden of Eden*—Hemingway enjoyed reversing traditional male/female roles in their sexual relationship. The women Hemingway chose were anything but traditional women of the early twentieth century, and there is ample evidence that his relationships with these women stretched the bounds of the conventional.

Scholars reading Hemingway today, unlike those of earlier generations, view his works through the lens of these revelations about the context of his life and the role gender bending played in it. The articles that follow—from early reviews to current analyses—explore male and female roles in *The Sun Also Rises*, as well as examining gender issues in twenty-first-century America.

Chronology

1899

Ernest Miller Hemingway is born in Oak Park, Illinois, on July 21, the second of six children of Clarence Edmunds Hemingway, MD, and Grace Hall Hemingway, a talented singer and music teacher.

1900

Hemingway's parents first take him to their summer cottage Windemere at Lake Walloon in northern Michigan, near Petoskey. In later years, Ernest's father, a devoted outdoorsman, will introduce him to fishing and hunting and the lessons of nature. The northern Michigan landscape will be used in some of his most successful short stories featuring Nick Adams.

1913–17

Hemingway attends Oak Park and River Forest high schools; he writes for the school newspaper and literary magazine. He boxes, plays football, and runs track while in school but is not considered an outstanding athlete.

1917

Hemingway graduates from Oak Park High School. He is rejected by the army because of an eye injury sustained in boxing. He works as a cub reporter for the *Kansas City Star*. The 110 rules of the *Star* style sheet require him to avoid adjectives and use short sentences, vigorous English, and fresh phrases. He would later call his days at the *Star* invaluable training for a writer.

1918

Hemingway joins an American Red Cross ambulance unit assisting the Italian army during World War I. His legs are severely injured by mortar fragments and heavy machine-gun fire at Fossalta on midnight July 8, two weeks before his nineteenth birthday. He spends months recuperating in a Milan hospital; his romance with a nurse, Agnes von Kurowsky, will provide the inspiration for his novel *A Farewell to Arms.*

1919

Hemingway returns to the United States and receives a letter from Agnes informing him she is engaged to another. His parents urge him to go to college or get a job.

1920

Grace Hemingway banishes Ernest from Windemere shortly after his twenty-first birthday. He travels to Toronto, Ontario, Canada, and becomes a freelance writer for the *Toronto Daily Star.* He returns to Chicago to write for the monthly magazine *The Cooperative Commonwealth.* In Chicago he meets Sherwood Anderson, who encourages his writing efforts.

1921

Hemingway marries the twenty-eight-year-old Hadley Richardson on September 3 in Horton Bay, Michigan. In December, using Sherwood Anderson's written endorsement, he becomes the European correspondent for the *Toronto Daily Star.* With the benefit of Hadley's trust fund, Hemingway and his new wife move to Paris at year's end. There he becomes friends with Gertrude Stein, Ezra Pound, Pablo Picasso, and other prominent artists and writers.

1922

Stein reads a fragment of Hemingway's novel-in-progress and suggests, "Begin over again and concentrate." In December, Hadley takes a train to Lausanne, Switzerland, where Hemingway is on assignment, and in transit a thief steals her valise, which contains the manuscripts of virtually all of Hemingway's unpublished fiction.

1923

Hemingway makes his first trip to Pamplona, Spain, for the bullfights and becomes immersed in the culture of bullfighting. He returns to Toronto in time for the birth of his son John Hadley (Bumby) in October. He publishes a limited-edition volume, *Three Stories and Ten Poems*.

1924

Hemingway's *In Our Time*, thirty-two pages of miniatures, is published in Paris. Hemingway assists Ford Madox Ford in editing the *Transatlantic Review*, which prints "Indian Camp" and other early Hemingway stories.

1925

In Our Time, the U.S. edition, is published by Boni & Liveright; it includes fourteen short stories plus the Parisian entries. Hemingway meets and befriends the slightly older and more established writer F. Scott Fitzgerald. He travels to Spain with Hadley, novelist Harold Loeb, Englishwoman Lady Duff Twysden and her fiancé Pat Guthrie, among others, for the Fiesta of San Fermin. Several of the events of this trip will be referred to in *The Sun Also Rises*, and several of the characters in the novel are said to be loosely based on these acquaintances.

1926

Hemingway's *The Torrents of Spring*, a satiric attack on his former mentor, Sherwood Anderson, is published in May. *The Sun Also Rises* is released in October to mostly glowing reviews. Hemingway is hailed as the defining writer of his "lost generation."

1927

Hemingway divorces Hadley and marries Pauline Pfeiffer, a wealthy American and devout Catholic working as a fashion writer; he converts to Catholicism. His short story collection

Men Without Women, which includes "Hills Like White Elephants" and "The Killers," is published.

1928

Hemingway moves with Pauline to Key West, Florida, where their son Patrick is born. Hemingway's father, beset by health and financial problems, commits suicide. Hemingway begins an affair with Martha Gellhorn, a journalist and writer.

1929

A Farewell to Arms, Hemingway's first major commercial success, is published; eighty thousand copies are sold in four months, despite (or possibly abetted by) the city of Boston's censorship of the serialized version in *Scribner's* magazine.

1931

Hemingway's son Gregory Hancock is born.

1932

Death in the Afternoon, Hemingway's lengthy essay on bullfighting, is published.

1933

Hemingway's *Winner Take Nothing*, a collection of fourteen stories including "A Clean, Well-Lighted Place," is published. He goes on safari to Africa, the setting for his two long stories "The Snows of Kilimanjaro" and "The Short Happy Life of Frances Macomber" (both published in 1936).

1935

Hemingway's *Green Hills of Africa*, an account of his safari adventures, is published.

1936–1937

Hemingway travels to Spain to cover the Spanish Civil War for the North American Newspaper Alliance. There he works on a propaganda film, *The Spanish Earth*, and donates funds to the Loyalist cause. He publishes *To Have and Have Not*, three interconnected stories.

1938

Hemingway's *The Fifth Column and the First Forty-Nine Stories* is published.

1939

Hemingway travels to Cuba to begin writing a novel on the Spanish Civil War. Martha Gellhorn follows him, renting a nearby house.

1940

For Whom the Bell Tolls, based on Hemingway's experiences in the Spanish Civil War, is published and dedicated to Gellhorn. An immediate success, it is his last novel for a decade. Pauline divorces him; he marries Martha Gellhorn in Sun Valley, Idaho, and moves with her to Havana, Cuba.

1942

Hemingway's *Men at War*, a collection of war stories, is published. He proposes to the American Embassy that he set up a private counterintelligence agency and he outfits his boat, the *Pilar*, to hunt German submarines in the Caribbean at the beginning of World War II.

1942–1945

Hemingway covers World War II in Europe as a newspaper and magazine correspondent. He observes D-Day—the Normandy invasion of June 6, 1944, by the Allies that led to the defeat of the German forces—firsthand and attaches himself to the Twenty-second Regiment, Fourth Infantry Division, for operations leading to the liberation of Paris and the Battle of Hürtgenwald. He begins an affair with Mary Welsh, an American journalist.

1944

Hemingway divorces Martha Gellhorn and marries Mary Welsh in Havana, Cuba.

1947

Hemingway receives the Bronze Star for war service during 1944.

1950

Hemingway's *Across the River and Into the Trees*, a romance, is published and critically savaged.

1953

Hemingway receives the Pulitzer Prize for his phenomenally successful novel *The Old Man and the Sea*. He returns to Africa for a safari with Mary.

1954

In January, Hemingway is severely injured in two successive plane crashes in Africa and is erroneously reported dead. He is awarded the Nobel Prize in Literature for "forceful and style-making mastery of the art of modern narration."

1960

Hemingway moves with Mary to Ketchum, Idaho. He suffers a nervous breakdown and enters the Mayo Clinic, where he undergoes electroshock therapy treatments.

1961

Beset by declining health, depression, and paranoia, early on the morning of July 2 Hemingway commits suicide by a gunshot to the head; he is buried in Sun Valley, Idaho.

1964

Hemingway's *A Moveable Feast* is published. It contains vivid and occasionally nasty sketches of those Hemingway knew in Paris during the 1920s, including Stein and Fitzgerald.

1970

Hemingway's *Islands in the Stream*, a semiautobiographical novel about a painter named Thomas Hudson and his family, is published.

1972

Hemingway's *The Nick Adams Stories*, which includes some previously unpublished stories and fragments, is published.

1980

The Hemingway Collection at the John F. Kennedy Library in Boston is opened to the public.

1981

Ernest Hemingway: Selected Letters, edited by Carlos Baker, is published.

1986

The Garden of Eden, a heavily edited and compressed version of Hemingway's last unfinished manuscript about love affairs between two women and one man, is published.

Social Issues in Literature

CHAPTER 1

Background on Ernest Hemingway

The Life of Ernest Hemingway

James Nagel

In his biographical and critical essay on Ernest Hemingway, James Nagel traces the chronology of the author's life, demonstrating how Hemingway wove some of the more dramatic events of his life into his writings. Hemingway, who was living in Paris following World War I, wrote of American expatriates in The Sun Also Rises. *Nagel considers the genius of the book to be in its sympathetic portrayal of the characters who were members of what Gertrude Stein termed the "lost generation." Jake Barnes has been damaged by the war, and because of the wound he bears, he is doomed to forever be a spectator at life, not an active participant. Nevertheless, Nagel contends, he is an honorable man who behaves decently in the novel. James Nagel is the Edison Distinguished Professor of English at the University of Georgia and the author of numerous works of literary criticism, including* Ernest Hemingway: The Oak Park Legacy.

Ernest Hemingway is one of the most celebrated and most controversial of American writers. He is seen variously as a sensitive and dedicated artist and as a hedonistic adventurer, as a literary poseur and as the stylistic genius of the century. His personal life has become so involved with his work that the two are virtually inseparable in scholarly inquiry: critics persist, with some justification, in reading characters in his works as "real" people and in assuming that events and attitudes in the fiction directly correspond with those in Hemingway's personal life. Hemingway was a strong man of definite opinion, who lived a vigorous life devoted to artistic creation and to active participation in the world. He was said to fill a room the moment he walked into it, and in those around him he inspired something close to hero worship. . . .

James Nagel, "Ernest Hemingway," in *Dictionary of Literary Biography, vol. 9: American Novelists, 1910–1945*, Belmont, CA: Gale Research Company, 1981. Reproduced by permission of Gale, a part of Cengage Learning.

His behavior inspired admiration in some people and astonishment and dismay in others, including his parents, but no matter what his stature as a person, his position as a writer of enormous talent and influence is well established.

The Early Years

Ernest Miller Hemingway was born in Oak Park, Illinois, the second child of Dr. Clarence Hemingway, a general practitioner, and Grace Hall Hemingway who had once aspired to an operatic career. In his youth his mother cultivated his interest in the arts, particularly in music and painting, and his father developed his natural love of sport and outdoor life. His father was a stern disciplinarian who insisted that his children adhere to Christian principles and decorum, and he demanded that things be done "properly." As a boy Ernest led an active life participating, without great distinction, in swimming, football, and boxing despite some limitations in coordination and in the sight of his left eye. While still in high school he began writing journalistic pieces and poems for the school newspaper and experimenting with stories. Although writing never came easily for him, he was apparently deeply interested in it at an early age.

After he graduated from Oak Park High School in 1917 he was given a junior position on the *Kansas City Star*, a leading newspaper of the period. The *Star* had developed a stylebook for its reporters that required the forming of direct, vigorous, declarative sentences, a practice that had a permanent influence on Hemingway's style. This period of his life ended in May 1918 when he volunteered for war duty with the Red Cross ambulance corps and left for service on the Italian front. There, on 8 July, after only a few weeks of service, he was hit by both mortar and machine-gun fire, treated in a Milan hospital and decorated as the first American wounded in Italy, and returned home to Oak Park a celebrity in an Italian officer's cape. In the long months of convalescence with his family, he turned to writing short stories based on his experiences. At other times he camped and fished in northern Michigan where his family had a cottage and where he had spent a good portion of his youth.

Eventually, however, Hemingway was forced by his parents to seek remunerative employment. By chance he was offered a position in Toronto in 1920 as companion to a lame boy of eighteen, a situation which led to his introduction to the *Toronto Star*. Although he was not given a job as a reporter, he was allowed to write articles at space rates, and after his marriage in 1921 to Hadley Richardson he was able to arrange a correspondent post with the newspaper, filing stories from Paris and other points in Europe. Paris was a highly artistic and inspiring environment for a beginning writer, for living on the Left Bank were many of the best writers in English, among them James Joyce, Ezra Pound, Gertrude Stein, and Ford Madox Ford.

Since he was writing only occasional pieces for the *Star*, Hemingway had time to devote to his own literary development, and he filled his notebooks with poems and impressionistic vignettes, working always for concentration and sharp, evocative descriptions. Unfortunately for literary historians, most of these early efforts were lost when his valise was stolen from a train compartment, but what remains indicates clearly the development of his basic principles of narration: leaving key elements of plot out of a story but contriving to have them affect the reader nonetheless; developing a plot on two levels simultaneously, one explicit and one implicit; restricting the narrative perspective to objective descriptions and matters of fact that a sensitive reader could use to infer the psychological conflicts at the heart of the story. In these years Hemingway had difficulties in getting his fiction published, but he had early success with "My Old Man," a story heavily influenced by Sherwood Anderson's work, and with "Out of Season" and "Up in Michigan," stories more uniquely his own. These stories appeared along with a selection of his poetry in *Three Stories & Ten Poems*, published by Robert McAlmon's Contact Publishing Company in Paris in 1923, in an edition of 300 copies. In the following year William Bird's Three Mountain Press published *In Our Time* in Paris in a limited edition of only 170 copies. The volume is made up of eighteen brief, impressionistic prose vignettes that vividly portray dramatic episodes. In 1925 this volume was enlarged and was published in New York by Boni & Liveright as *In Our Time* which contained not only the brief sketches of the earlier volume but fifteen of Hemingway's finest stories, including "Indian Camp," "Soldier's Home," and "Big Two-Hearted River."

In 1926, Scribners published Hemingway's *The Torrents of Spring*, a parody of Sherwood Anderson's *Dark Laughter*. There is reason to believe that he used this satirical novel to break his contract with Boni & Liveright, who also published the better-known Anderson, to clear the way for a new contractual agreement with Scribners. In any event, Boni & Liveright refused the novel and Hemingway published it with Scribners, a relationship he maintained to the end of his life.

The Sun Also Rises Establishes Hemingway's Reputation

By 1926 Hemingway had been praised by such illustrious literary figures as F. Scott Fitzgerald, Gertrude Stein, and Sherwood Anderson. He was regarded as a young author with a stirring vitality and a unique style, a promising writer from whom more would be heard. With the publication in October of that year of *The Sun Also Rises*, a novel based on his years in Paris and Spain after the war, the period of apprenticeship closed, and Hemingway emerged from it an established writer of international acclaim whose first major effort equaled or eclipsed anything written by his mentors. The publication of his short stories in *Men Without Women* (1927) added to his growing reputation. But his professional success coincided with familial turmoil; in the fall of 1926 Hemingway had left Hadley Hemingway and their son Bumby, born in 1923, for Pauline Pfeiffer, a woman he had come to know in Paris. They decided to leave Europe, eventually settling in Key West, Florida, in the fall of 1928. Thus began a peripatetic domestic existence for Hemingway that was eventually to involve Montana, Idaho, Cuba, Africa, Spain, Italy, and various other points around the world. The year 1928 brought near-tragedy and death: in June, Pauline Hemingway, small of stature, gave birth to a son, Patrick, by a traumatic cesarean section; in December, Dr. Hemingway, suffering from diabetes and related complications, committed suicide with a revolver. The incident of Patrick's birth Hemingway re-created, with a tragic conclusion, in *A Farewell to Arms* (1929), his first genuine commercial success, selling 80,000 copies within four months of publication. This novel treated the experiences of Frederic Henry on the Italian front in the First World War and his eventual desertion to Switzerland with Catherine Barkley, only to have Catherine die in childbirth. In 1931 the last of Hemingway's children was born, his third son, Gregory, again by cesarean section.

The Years of Adventure

The 1930s were a decade of personal adventure, and Hemingway hunted in the American West and in Africa, fished the Gulf Stream of Cuba and Florida, and covered the Spanish Civil War as a correspondent. He wrote an extended essay on bullfighting, *Death in the Afternoon* (1932), which is still considered a valuable treatment of its subject. A collection of stories, *Winner Take Nothing*, appeared in 1933. *Green Hills of Africa*, an account of adventures on safari, was published in 1935 and was followed, in 1937, by *To Have and Have Not*, one of the weakest of Hemingway's novels. But his most no

Ernest Hemingway AP Images

table involvement during this period was his work on behalf of the Loyalist cause in Spain. Ostensibly a reporter covering the war for the North American Newspaper Alliance, in 1937–1938 Hemingway helped raise money for medical supplies and ambulances by speaking in the United States against the spread of fascism in Europe, and he helped with the production of *The Spanish Earth*, a pro-Loyalist film designed to enlist foreign aid for their cause. Out of this experience as well he wrote a play, *The Fifth Column*, which was published in 1938 along with *The First Forty-nine Stories*. But the most important work to come from his time in Spain was *For Whom the*

Bell Tolls (1940), a brilliant novel about Robert Jordan, an American Spanish instructor who fights with the Loyalist forces.

The period before and during World War II brought changes to Hemingway's life. In 1940 he divorced Pauline Pfeiffer and married Martha Gellhorn, a vibrant and determined reporter with whom he had covered battles in Spain. Together they established their home in the Cuban village of San Francisco de Paula near Havana, where Hemingway was to live most of the rest of his life. With the outbreak of the war in Europe he outfitted his fishing boat Pilar as an antisubmarine vessel and for nearly two years searched, unsuccessfully, for German submarines in the Gulf, events later given fictional treatment in *Islands in the Stream* (1970), a novel published after his death. In 1944 he went to England as a correspondent for Collier's, accompanying Martha Hemingway, who had gone the year before but had returned to be with her husband. Hemingway flew missions with the R. A. F. [Royal Air Force], covered the landing in Normandy, and attached himself to Allied forces in France during the remainder of the war, sometimes serving as scout and interrogator as well as journalist, activities which led to his decoration with the Bronze Star. This period also saw his gradual estrangement from his wife and his deepening involvement with Mary Welsh, also a journalist covering the war, and after his third divorce they were married in Havana in 1946.

The Later Years and the Nobel Prize

Back in Cuba, Hemingway worked on a novel about a colonel named Richard Cantwell who is involved with a beautiful young woman in Venice just before his death. Entitled *Across the River and Into the Trees*, the book seemed nearly a parody of Hemingway's characteristic style and themes, and it was a disappointment to nearly everyone when it appeared in 1950. He had much better fortune with *The Old Man and the Sea* in

1952, which was not only a commercial success but won the Pulitzer Prize. This honor was followed in 1954 by the award of the Nobel Prize for Literature. Beyond these literary triumphs, Hemingway's adventurous life continued with an African safari with Mary Hemingway in 1953, during which he suffered serious head and abdominal injuries in a plane crash, and with a period in Spain covering the rivalry between two famous matadors, Antonio Ordóñez and Luis Dominguin, the account of which was published as "The Dangerous Summer." After the coming to power of Fidel Castro in Cuba, Hemingway moved his home permanently to Ketchum, Idaho, where he continued work on a series of sketches of life in Paris during the early years of his career, a volume published after his death as *A Moveable Feast* (1964). But age was difficult for him. A lifetime of dangerous physical adventure had taken its toll in numerous injuries, including several concussions, many of them severe. In addition he was suffering from hypertension, mild diabetes, and depression, for which he was given electric shock treatments. He became confused, suspicious, and aggressively suicidal; he agonized that he could not write, and he was convinced that he was being watched by government agents. After his release from the Mayo Clinic in Minnesota, he returned home to Idaho, and on 2 July 1961, in the early morning, selected a favorite shotgun and committed suicide. . . .

Book One of *The Sun Also Rises*

Hemingway's reputation rests primarily on his major novels, which are regarded by many scholars as among the finest in American literature. The first of these, *The Sun Also Rises*, caused a sensation when it appeared in 1926. It quickly became a celebrated statement of the views of the "lost generation," views that combined disillusionment with traditional values, brought on in part by World War I, with a new hedonistic attitude, exemplified by the female protagonist, Lady

Brett Ashley. It was the first major depiction of the lives of American expatriates in Paris in the 1920s, and American adolescents responded to it immediately, imitating its dialogue and tone of hopeless love; young women cut their hair and adopted clothing inspired by Brett; young men came to think of themselves as being part of the aftermath of the war, even if they were too young to have participated in it.

The novel is narrated in a spare and idiomatic style by Jake Barnes, an American correspondent in Paris who was severely wounded in the war and has been left impotent. As he reveals later, he is in love with Brett, and she with him; because their love cannot be consummated, they find it torture to be together. But their love is the most stable relationship in the novel, and in times of trouble they inevitably come to one another for comfort. The early sections of the novel are deceptively celebrative in tone, however, concentrating on the fervor of expatriate life in Paris. Jake tells about Robert Cohn, a young Jewish writer from Princeton who is living with Frances Clyne, a possessive and insecure woman he quickly tires of. When Jake impulsively picks up a prostitute, he reveals to her that he is "sick" and she indicates that she is too; indeed, everyone is "sick." There is truth in her pronouncement, for nearly all of Jake's friends in Paris are seeking desperately for some unattainable happiness or fulfillment: Brett in romantic conquest, Cohn in romantic novels or, later, in his affair with Brett, and others of the group in their frantic celebration. Even the wealthy Greek, Count Mippipopolous, who carries arrow wounds from earlier wars, shares in this apparently joyous revel. The serious underside of this life is revealed largely through Jake's psychological turmoil, a vestige of the trauma of the war, that at times nearly incapacitates him. He suffers from insomnia; when his "head starts to work" he is emotionally unstable, crying in the night and remembering how he met Brett in England when she was a nurse. Brett, too, has her troubles: her fiance died of dysentery during the war;

she made a bad marriage to acquire a title; now she plans to marry Mike Campbell, a Scottish bankrupt who cannot control his drinking and has no hopes for the future.

Book Two of *The Sun Also Rises*

The second section of the novel is more dramatic and more positive. The central action covers the journey of Jake and his friends to Spain for the fiesta and bullfighting; on the way, Jake and Bill Gorton stop for a few days in Basque country to fish for trout. Here, in a quiet, natural setting, Bill and Jake relax and fish and engage in humorous banter touching on all the serious themes of the novel: religion, expatriation, sex, love, and the aftermath of the war. They are joined in their fishing by a generous and sensitive Englishman named Harris who, along with Bill, is one of the few positive portraits in the novel. Leaving the Basque region, Jake and Bill go on to Pamplona for the running of the bulls and the fiesta, during which the principal drama is the courtship of Brett. Before the fiesta, Brett had run off to San Sebastián with Robert Cohn for a romantic weekend. Now Cohn feels a proprietary interest in her despite her engagement to Mike Campbell and her growing attraction for Pedro Romero, a young bullfighter. Jake, an aficionado, a person who loves and truly understands bullfighting and its ritual, explains the proceedings to Brett and the others. However, he loses the respect of Montoya, another aficionado, when he violates the code by introducing Brett to Pedro. The competition for Brett finally erupts into a fight, with Robert Cohn knocking down Jake and Mike and then beating Pedro badly without being able to make him quit. Despite his injuries, Pedro fights the bulls heroically the next day and then runs off with Brett. The fun and adventure of the fiesta has, by its conclusion, become grimly unromantic.

Book Three of *The Sun Also Rises*

The final section of the novel is very brief and deals with the denouement of the fiesta. As the group disperses, Jake goes to

San Sebastián to recover. There he gets a telegram from Brett in Madrid. She has left Pedro and needs Jake's help. He arrives after an all-night train ride to discover that Brett left Pedro out of conscience, not wanting to ruin him. The dialogue of this section is especially memorable, as when Brett says to Jake: "You know it makes one feel rather good deciding not to be a bitch." "Yes." "It's sort of what we have instead of God." Jake and Brett then drive off in a taxi dreaming about the life they might have had together: "Yes," Jake says, "Isn't it pretty to think so?"

The novel ends where it began, with Brett and Jake trapped in a hopeless love for each other. None of the major problems have been resolved, none of the characters have achieved any sort of lasting fulfillment: they are truly of the "lost genera-tion." Hemingway prefaced his novel with two quotations: "You are all a lost generation," attributed to Gertrude Stein, and a passage from Ecclesiastes that begins "one generation passeth away, and another generation cometh; but the earth abideth forever. . . ." Stein's remark points to the disillusion-ment and emptiness of the novel and to the existential notion that life is fundamentally pointless and absurd, ideas well de-veloped by the events of the novel. The biblical passage has a much more subtle relationship to the novel in its promise of natural continuity and renewal, of a cycle of fortunes from conclusions to beginnings once again. Aside from the brief fishing trip, the vulnerable nobility of Pedro, the love between Brett and Jake, there is little optimism, but there is the sugges-tion that if the lives of this generation have been ruined by events beyond their control, there will nevertheless be another generation that may yet find meaning in their lives.

These themes owe their intensity to other factors in the novel, especially to Jake's understated yet effective narration. He is on the outside of the world he portrays, unable to par-ticipate fully in it, and yet he is an informed and perceptive recorder of its frenetic drama. Like Nick Adams [a character in stories collected in *In Our Time* and *The Nick Adams Stories*], he knows the proper codes of behavior, and he judges harshly those, like Robert Cohn, who do not. He has been physically and psychologically wounded in the war in ways that have irrevocably changed his life, but he is still a sensitive and prescient human being who matters enormously. Much of the skill of the novel is in its portraying so sympathetically the lives of a "lost" group of people who were intelligent and sentient and yet leading hopeless lives, who were in some way the victim of historical tragedies of epic force. In this sense, the characters of *The Sun Also Rises* epitomize a generation by portraying the anguish of the Western world over the European war, over the shattered illusion of peaceful order that had been irrevocably lost. . . .

Hemingway the Writer Will Endure

Hemingway's reputation will forever rest on an uneasy blending of the myth of his personal adventures with the artistic merit of his best fiction. But it is as artist that he deserves the attention of posterity. He was, without doubt, one of the finest prose stylists in English. He captured in stunning stories and novels the uncomfortable realities of his age and forced into public consciousness a realization of the brutalities of war and their lingering psychological effects. His stories of Nick Adams depict the adolescent agonies of a generation; his novels, especially *The Sun Also Rises*, *A Farewell to Arms*, and *For Whom the Bell Tolls*, record for all time the emotional turmoil of modern warfare and, in a larger sense, of modern life. And by concluding his career with *The Old Man and the Sea* he showed that even in the anguish of modern life there is nobility in human perseverance and dignity in devotion to performing a task well. Whatever failings he had as a man, and there were many, as a writer he was sometimes nearly perfect. It is the integrity of his craft, a richness beyond legend, that will forever endure.

Hemingway on Truth, Disillusionment, and the Hero

Contemporary Authors Online

This excerpt from an entry on Hemingway in Contemporary Authors Online *describes how his search for truth is reflected in both the subject matter and style of his writings. The quest for truth also led Hemingway to related explorations of morality and the disillusioning effect of war, both of which were portrayed in* The Sun Also Rises. *Out of the disillusionment, however, rise heroes who retain their qualities even in the face of defeat.*

"The writer's job is to tell the truth," Ernest Hemingway once said. When he was having difficulty writing he reminded himself of this, as he explained in his memoirs, *A Moveable Feast*. "I would stand and look out over the roofs of Paris and think, 'Do not worry. You have always written before and you will write now. All you have to do is write one true sentence. Write the truest sentence that you know.' So finally I would write one true sentence, and then go on from there. It was easy then because there was always one true sentence that I knew or had seen or had heard someone say."

Hemingway's personal and artistic quests for truth were directly related. As Earl Rovit noted: "More often than not, Hemingway's fictions seem rooted in his journeys into himself much more clearly and obsessively than is usually the case with major fiction writers. . . . His writing was his way of approaching his identity—of discovering himself in the projected metaphors of his experience. He believed that if he could see himself clear and whole, his vision might be useful to others who also lived in this world." . . .

Hemingway's search for truth and accuracy of expression is reflected in his terse, economical prose style, which is widely

Contemporary Authors Online, "Ernest (Miller) Hemingway," October 4, 2005. Reproduced by permission of Gale, a part of Cengage Learning.

acknowledged to be his greatest contribution to literature. What Frederick J. Hoffman called Hemingway's "esthetic of simplicity" involves a "basic struggle for absolute accuracy in making words correspond to experience." For Hemingway, William Barrett commented, "style was a moral act, a desperate struggle for moral probity amid the confusions of the world and the slippery complexities of one's own nature. To set things down simple and right is to hold a standard of rightness against a deceiving world."

In a discussion of Hemingway's style, Sheldon Norman Grebstein listed these characteristics: "first, short and simple sentence constructions, with heavy use of parallelism, which convey the effect of control, terseness, and blunt honesty; second, purged diction which above all eschews the use of bookish, latinate, or abstract words and thus achieves the effect of being heard or spoken or transcribed from reality rather than appearing as a construct of the imagination (in brief, verisimilitude); and third, skillful use of repetition and a kind of verbal counterpoint, which operate either by pairing or juxtaposing opposites, or else by running the same word or phrase through a series of shifting meanings and inflections." . . .

It is [an] organicism, [a] skillful blend of style and substance, that made Hemingway's works so successful, despite the fact that many critics have complained that he lacked vision. Hemingway avoided intellectualism because he thought it shallow and pretentious. His unique vision demanded the expression of emotion through the description of action rather than of passive thought. In *Death in the Afternoon*, Hemingway explained, "I was trying to write then and I found the greatest difficulty, aside from knowing truly what you really felt, rather than what you were supposed to feel, was to put down what really happened in action; what the actual things were which produced the emotion you experienced."

Hemingway worked as a newspaper correspondent throughout his life, developing a writing style that had an influence on his fiction. Here he poses with an American soldier in 1938 during his time reporting on the Spanish Civil War. AP Images.

Even morality, for Hemingway, was a consequence of action and emotion. He stated his moral code in *Death in the Afternoon*: "What is moral is what you feel good after and what is immoral is what you feel bad after." Lady Brett Ashley, in *The Sun Also Rises*, voices this pragmatic morality after she has decided to leave a young bullfighter, believing the break to be in his best interests. She says: "You know it makes one feel rather good deciding not to be a bitch.... It's sort of what we have instead of God."

Hemingway's perception of the world as devoid of traditional values and truths and instead marked by disillusionment and moribund idealism, is a characteristically twentieth-century vision. World War I was a watershed for Hemingway and his generation. As an ambulance driver in the Italian infantry, Hemingway had been severely wounded. The war experience affected him profoundly, as he told Malcolm Cowley. "In the first war I was hurt very badly; in the body, mind, and spirit, and also morally." The heroes of his novels were similarly wounded. According to Max Westbrook they "awake to a world gone to hell. World War I has destroyed belief in the goodness of national governments. The depression has isolated man from his natural brotherhood. Institutions, concepts, and insidious groups of friends and ways of life are, when accurately seen, a tyranny, a sentimental or propagandistic rationalization."

Both of Hemingway's first two major novels, *The Sun Also Rises* and *A Farewell to Arms*, were "primarily descriptions of a society that had lost the possibility of belief. They were dominated by an atmosphere of Gothic ruin, boredom, sterility and decay," John Aldridge wrote. "Yet if they had been nothing more than descriptions, they would inevitably have been as empty of meaning as the thing they were describing." While Alan Lebowitz contended that because the theme of despair "is always an end in itself, the fiction merely its transcription, . . . it is a dead end," Aldridge believed that Hemingway managed to save the novels by salvaging the characters' values and transcribing them "into a kind of moral network that linked them together in a unified pattern of meaning." . . .

The code by which Hemingway's heroes must live (Philip Young has termed them "code heroes") is contingent on the qualities of courage, self-control, and "grace under pressure." Irving Howe has described the typical Hemingway hero as a man "who is wounded but bears his wounds in silence, who is defeated but finds a remnant of dignity in an honest confrontation of defeat." Furthermore, the hero's great desire must be to "salvage from the collapse of social life a version of stoicism that can make suffering bearable; the hope that in direct physical sensation, the cold water of the creek in which one fishes or the purity of the wine made by Spanish peasants, there can be found an experience that can resist corruption."

Hemingway and the Test of Manhood

Irving Howe

In his obituary summing up Ernest Hemingway's life and work, Irving Howe writes of the difficulty of separating Hemingway the writer from Hemingway the man. He argues that Hemingway's great subject was not courage, as many critics suggest, but panic. Howe is critical of the later work of Hemingway, finding his first novel, The Sun Also Rises, *to be his finest. Howe points out that, in this early work, Hemingway writes of manhood—in the character of Jake Barnes—being put to the test and enduring with stoicism. Although Howe finds Hemingway's vision essentially narrow, he maintains there are times when his writing approached greatness. Howe was a professor of literature at City University of New York and a noted literary critic and founder of the literary quarterly* Dissent.

Now that he is dead and nothing remains but a few books and the problem of his dying, perhaps we should ask the simplest, most radical of questions: what was there in Hemingway's writing that enabled him to command the loyalty of a generation? Even those of us who disliked some of his work and most of his posture, why did we too feel compelled to acknowledge the strength and resonance of his voice?

Answering such questions can never be easy, and with Hemingway, master that he is of false leads and distracting personnae, it demands a touch of ruthlessness. The usual business of literary criticism will yield only limited returns, for if you were to spend the next decade studying the narrative techniques of his stories you would still be far from the

Irving Howe, "Hemingway: The Conquest of Panic," *The New Republic*, vol. 145, July 24, 1961, pp. 19–20. Copyright © 1961 by The New Republic, Inc. Reproduced by permission of *The New Republic*.

sources of his power. Most of his late work was bad, Papa gone soft, desperately in search of the image of self he had made in his youth. . . .

For the past twenty years the public Hemingway, who cannot after all be so readily separated from Hemingway, was a tiresome man. The old African hunter, the connoisseur of bulls, women and wars, the experience-dropper, was a show-off who had stopped watching the audience to see if it remained interested. . . .

Years earlier Hemingway had written, "Something happens to our good writers at a certain age. . . ." Yes; they devote the first half of their lives to imitating human experience and the second to parodying their imitation.

A Young Writer for the Young

But there was another Hemingway. He was always a young writer, and always a writer for the young. He published his best novel *The Sun Also Rises* in his mid-twenties and completed most of his great stories by the age of forty. He started a campaign of terror against the fixed vocabulary of literature, a purge of style and pomp, and in the name of naturalness he modelled a new artifice for tension. He was a short-breathed writer, whether in the novel or story. He struck past the barriers of culture and seemed to disregard the reticence of civilized relationships. He wrote for the nerves.

In his very first stories Hemingway struck straight to the heart of our nihilism, writing with that marvellous courage he then had, which allowed him to brush past received ideas and show Nick Adams [hero of the Nick Adams stories featured in *In Our Time* and later in their own collection entitled *The Nick Adams Stories*] alone, bewildered, afraid and bored, Nick Adams finding his bit of peace through fishing with an exact salvaging ritual in the big two-hearted river Hemingway struck straight to the heart of our nihilism through stories about people who have come to the end of the line, who no longer know what to do or where to turn: nihilism not as an idea or a sentiment, but as an encompassing condition of moral disarray in which one has lost those tacit impulsions which permit life to continue and suddenly begins to ask questions that would better be left unasked. There is a truth which makes our faith in human existence seem absurd, and no one need contemplate it for very long: Hemingway, in his early writing did. Nick Adams, Jake Barnes, Lady Brett, Frederic Henry [hero of *A Farewell to Arms*] and then the prizefighters, matadors, rich Americans and failed writers: all are at the edge, almost ready to surrender and be done with it, yet holding on to whatever fragment of morale, whatever scrap of honor, they can. Theirs is the heroism of people who have long ago given up the idea of being heroic and wish only to get by without being too messy.

Hemingway and the Problem of Fear

It has been said that Hemingway, obsessed with the problem of fear, sought in his fiction for strategies to overcome it; and that is true, but only partly so. Hemingway was not so foolish as to suppose that fear can finally be overcome: all his best stories, from "Fifty Grand" to "The Short Happy Life of Francis Macomber" are concerned to improvise a momentary truce in the hopeless encounter with fear. Hemingway touched upon something deeper, something that broke forth in his fiction as the most personal and lonely kind of experience but was formed by the pressure of 20th Century history. His great subject, I think, was panic, the panic that follows, so to speak, upon the dissolution of nihilism into the blood-stream of consciousness, the panic that finds unbearable the thought of the next minute and its succession by the minute after that. And we all know his experience, even if, unlike Jake Barnes, we can sleep at night we know it because it is part of modern life, perhaps of any life, but also because Hemingway drove it fearlessly into our awareness.

Hemingway and his third wife Martha Gellhorn, a writer and war correspondent, are pictured on the terrace of the Sun Valley Lodge. AP Images.

But there was more. Hemingway's early fiction made his readers turn in upon themselves with the pain of measurement and consider the question of their sufficiency as men. He touched the quick of our anxieties, and for the moment of his excellence he stood ready to face whatever he saw. The compulsive stylization of his prose was a way of letting the language tense and retense, group and regroup, while beneath it the panic that had taken hold of the characters and then of the reader kept spreading inexorably. The prose served both as barrier and principle of contrast to that shapelessness which is panic by definition, and through its very tautness allowed the reader finally to establish some distance and then perhaps compassion.

This Hemingway forced us to ask whether as men we had retained any thrust and will, any unbreakable pride. He asked this question in the most fundamental sexual way, moving from the desperateness of *The Sun Also Rises* to the comforts but also final return to bleakness in *A Farewell to Arms*, from the sleeping-bag fantasia—with [the character] Maria as a sort of Fayaway [the innocent character in Herman Melville's *Typee*] with politics—of *For Whom the Bell Tolls* to the boozy ruminations of *Across the River and Into the Trees*. But he also asked the question in other ways.

The poet John Berryman once said that we live in a culture where a man can go through his entire life without having once to discover whether he is a coward. Hemingway forced his readers to consider such possibilities, and through the clenched shape of his stories he kept insisting that no one can escape, moments of truth come to all of us. Fatalistic as they often seem, immersed in images of violence and death, his stories are actually incitements to personal resistance and renewal. Reading them, one felt stirred to a stronger sense—if not of one's possible freedom—then at least of one's possible endurance and companionship in stoicism.

Hemingway's vision was narrow. It was, as an Italian critic has remarked, "a brilliant half-vision of life," in which a whole range of behavior, not least of all the behavior of man thinking, was left out. But there were moments when he wrote with a sudden enlarged sensibility, so that one forgot the limits of his stance and style, feeling that here, for these few pages, one was in the presence of a great writer. There is a little story called "A Clean Well-Lighted Place" and a passage in that story where the older waiter explains to the younger one that he must be patient with the homeless men sitting in the café, because everyone needs a clean well-lighted place in which to stare at his aloneness. I cannot imagine that this story will ever be forgotten.

The Sun Also Rises and Male and Female Roles

The Sun Also Rises Criticizes Postwar Society

Edmund Wilson

Edmund Wilson was one of the most important literary critics of the twentieth century. As a managing editor of Vanity Fair, *writer for the* New Republic, *and book review editor for the* New Yorker, *he was influential in launching the careers of F. Scott Fitzgerald, Vladimir Nabokov, John Dos Passos, and Ernest Hemingway. In the following excerpt from his seminal work* The Wound and the Bow, *Wilson examines the code that governs Hemingway's male and female characters in* The Sun Also Rises. *He points out that in this novel and Hemingway's other works from that period, Hemingway offers an astute commentary on society, expressing the "romantic disillusion" of the era. Wilson's criticism of* The Sun Also Rises *was noteworthy for the unequivocal position he took about Lady Brett Ashley, describing her as "an exclusively destructive force." Wilson asserts that the depiction of Brett reveals Hemingway's lack of sympathy toward women.*

Note: Bracketed text has been inserted by the editors.

The next fishing trip is strikingly different. Perhaps the first [taken by Nick Adams in stories collected in *In Our Time*] had been an idealization. Is it possible to attain to such sensuous bliss merely through going alone into the woods: smoking, fishing, and eating, with no thought about anyone else or about anything one has ever done or will ever be obliged to do? At any rate, today, in *The Sun Also Rises*, all the things that are wrong with human life are there on the holiday, too—

though one tries to keep them back out of the foreground and to occupy one's mind with the trout, caught now in a stream of the Pyrenees, and with the kidding of the friend from the States. The feeling of insecurity has deepened. The young American now appears in a seriously damaged condition: he has somehow been incapacitated sexually through wounds received in the war. He is in love with one of those international sirens who flourished in the cafés of the post-war period and whose ruthless and uncontrollable infidelities, in such a circle as that depicted by Hemingway, have made any sort of security impossible for the relations between women and men. The lovers of such a woman turn upon and rend one another because they are powerless to make themselves felt by *her*.

The casualties of the bullfight at Pamplona [Spain], to which these young people have gone for the *fiesta*, only reflect the blows and betrayals of demoralized human beings out of hand. What is the tiresome lover with whom the lady has just been off on a casual escapade, and who is unable to understand that he has been discarded, but the man who, on his way to the bullring, has been accidentally gored by the bull? The young American who tells the story is the only character who keeps up standards of conduct, and he is prevented by his disability from dominating and directing the woman, who otherwise, it is intimated, might love him. Here the membrane of the style has been stretched taut to convey the vibrations of these qualms. The dry sunlight and the green summer landscapes have been invested with a sinister quality which must be new in literature. One enjoys the sun and the green as one enjoys suckling pigs and Spanish wine, but the uneasiness and apprehension are undruggable.

Yet one can catch hold of a code in all the drunkenness and the social chaos. 'Perhaps as you went along you did learn something,' Jake, the hero, reflects at one point. 'I did not care what it was all about. All I wanted to know was how to live in it. Maybe if you found out how to live in it you learned from that what it was all about.' 'Everybody behaves badly. Give them the proper chance,' he says later to Lady Brett.

"You wouldn't behave badly." Brett looked at me.' In the end, she sends for Jake, who finds her alone in a hotel. She has left her regular lover for a young bullfighter, and this boy has for the first time inspired her with a respect which has restrained her from 'ruining' him: 'You know it makes one feel rather good deciding not to be a bitch.' We suffer and we make suffer, and everybody loses out in the long run; but in the meantime we can lose with honor.

* * *

This Hemingway of the middle twenties—*The Sun Also Rises* came out in '26—expressed the romantic disillusion and set the favorite pose for the period. It was the moment of gallantry in heartbreak, grim and nonchalant banter, and heroic dissipation. The great watchword was 'Have a drink'; and in the bars of New York and Paris the young people were getting to talk like Hemingway.

* * *

The emotion which principally comes through in *Francis Macomber* and *The Snows of Kilimanjaro*—as it figures also in *The Fifth Column*—is a growing antagonism to women. Looking back, one can see at this point that the tendency has been there all along.

* * *

Brett in *The Sun Also Rises* is an exclusively destructive force: she might be a better woman if she were mated with Jake, the American; but actually he is protected against her and is in a sense revenging his own sex being unable to do anything for her sexually.

* * *

Going back over Hemingway's books today [in 1929] we can see clearly what an error of the politicos it was to accuse him of an indifference to society. His whole work is a criticism of society: he has responded to every pressure of the moral atmosphere of the time, as it is felt at the roots of human relations, with a sensitivity almost unrivaled. Even his preoccupation with licking the gang in the next block and being known as the best basketball player in high school has its meaning in the present epoch. After all, whatever is done in the world, political as well as athletic, depends on personal courage and strength. With Hemingway, courage and strength are always thought of in physical terms, so that he tends to give the impression that the bullfighter who can take it and dish it out is more of a man than any other kind of man, and that the sole duty of the revolutionary socialist is to get the counter-revolutionary gang before they get him.

But ideas, however correct, will never prevail by themselves: there must be people who are prepared to stand or fall with them, and the ability to act on principle is still subject to the same competitive laws which operate in sporting contests and sexual relations. Hemingway has expressed with genius the terrors of the modern man at the danger of losing control of his world, and he has also, within his scope, provided his own kind of antidote. This antidote, paradoxically, is almost entirely moral. Despite Hemingway's preoccupation with physical contests, his heroes are almost always defeated physically, nervously, practically: their victories are moral ones. He himself, when he trained himself stubbornly in his unconventional unmarketable art in a Paris which had other fashions, gave the prime example of such a victory; and if he has sometimes, under the menace of the general panic, seemed on the point of going to pieces as an artist, he has always pulled himself together the next moment.

The Moral and the Neurotic Are Two Sets of Characters in *The Sun Also Rises*

Carlos Baker

Carlos Baker, considered Ernest Hemingway's official biographer, contends that the writer rejected the "lost generation" label both for himself and for his generation and finds it ironic that so many critics consider The Sun Also Rises *to be the bible of the lost generation. Baker divides the characters in the book into two camps. One group, led by Jake Barnes and including Bill Gorton and Pedro Romero, is healthy and moral, if wounded. The other group, led by Brett Ashley and including Robert Cohn and Mike Campbell, is neurotic and spiritually bankrupt. Baker argues that the book can be read as a study of the tension of manly valor pitted against emotional and spiritual emptiness. Baker was a Woodrow Wilson Professor of Literature at Princeton University and the author of numerous critical and biographical works, including* Ernest Hemingway: A Life Story.

The Sun Also Rises was the means Hemingway chose to declare himself out of the alleged "lostness" of a generation whose vagaries he chronicled. In 1922 he had recorded his humorous scorn for the artistic scum of Montparnasse. Now, through Jake Barnes, he withdrew to the position of a detached observer looking on at aimless revels which at once amused him and left him sick at heart. For it is one view of Jake that he is an imperturbable and damaged Hamlet. . . .

In order to write his book it had been necessary for Hemingway to dissociate himself in a moral sense from the very idea of lostness. He might tell [F. Scott] Fitzgerald that *The*

Carlos Baker, "The Wastelanders," in *Hemingway: The Writer as Artist*. 3rd ed., Princeton, NJ: Princeton University Press, 1963, pp. 75–93.

Sun Also Rises was "a hell of a sad story" whose only instruction was "how people go to hell." But the point of the book for him, as he wrote [editor Maxwell] Perkins, was "that the earth abideth forever." He had "a great deal of fondness and admiration for the earth, and not a hell of a lot for my generation," and he cared "little about vanities." The book was not meant to be "a hollow or bitter satire, but a damn tragedy with the earth abiding forever as the hero."

The reading public in general did not appear to understand the point or the degree of dissociation between the artist and his characters. One heard that Jake Barnes was a modified self-portrait of Hemingway, dripping with self-pity, when in fact Hemingway was facing the hazards of *la vie humaine* [human life] with courage and a reasonably light heart, as, for that matter, was Jake Barnes. "There really is, to me anyway, very great glamour in life—and places and all sorts of things and I would like sometime to get it into the stuff," he wrote to Maxwell Perkins. "I've known some very wonderful people who even though they were going directly to the grave (which is what makes any story a tragedy if carried out until the end) managed to put up a very fine performance enroute." It ought to have been plain to discerning readers that Jake Barnes, Bill Gorton, and Pedro Romero were solid—if slightly beat-up—citizens of the republic. They were not lost. They refused to surrender to neuroses like those which beset Robert Cohn, Brett Ashley, and Mike Campbell. And three lost neurotics do not make a lost generation.

It was one of the ironies that Hemingway, having rejected the lost-generation tag both for himself and for his generation, should find his first book widely accepted as Exhibit A of "lost-generationism." Another conspicuous irony was that most readers found Brett and her little circle of drinking-companions so fascinating as to overshadow the idea of the abiding earth as the true hero of the book. Hemingway's love and admiration for the natural earth was certainly quite clearly projected. Any beat-up Antaeus who could gain strength and sanity from contact with the earth was a kind of hero in his eyes, as one saw in the portraits of Barnes and Gorton and Romero. Yet all eyes were drawn towards Brett—possibly by the odd mixture of irony and pity, of condemnation and admiration, with which she was treated.

Jake, Bill, and Romero Form Moral Center

Hemingway had told Perkins that he cared little about the vanities. *The Sun Also Rises* was one of the proofs of that statement. The title comes from the first chapter of Ecclesiastes. It is useful to recognize the strong probability that the moral of the novel is derived from the same book: "All is vanity and vexation of spirit." All is vanity, at any rate, along the Vanity Fair of the Boulevard Montparnasse where the novelist introduces his people and completes his preliminary exposition. "Everybody's sick," says Jake's little *poule* [prostitute] in the Parisian horsecab. The novel goes on to prove that if you concentrate on a certain segment of expatriated society, she is very nearly right. All is vanity at the Pamplona fiesta when Cohn and Campbell, moody and sullen among the empty bottles, bicker over Brett while she makes off with the matador. All is vanity when Jake concludes this little chapter of social history in a taxi on the Gran Via of Madrid. "Oh, Jake," cries Brett, "we could have had such a damned good time together." "Yes," Jake answers, closing the volume. "Isn't it pretty to think so?"

The novel contains, however, enough bright metal to bring out by contrast the special darkness of the sullen ground. We are meant to understand that all is vanity—except the things that are not vain. The moral norm of the book is a healthy and almost boyish innocence of spirit, and it is carried by Jake Barnes, Bill Gorton, and Pedro Romero. Against this norm, in the central antithesis of the novel, is ranged the sick abnormal "vanity" of the Ashley-Campbell-Cohn triangle.

Long before the middle of the book, a reader who is reasonably sensitive to changes in tone may discover that he has been silently forced into a choice between two sets of moral and emotional atmospheres. Something tarnished is opposed to something bright; vanity is challenged by sanity; a world of mean and snarled disorder is set off against a world clear of entangling alliances. The whole mood of the novel brightens, for example, when the men-without-women, Jake Barnes and Bill Gorton, climb to the roof of the bus which will take them to Burguete in the Pyrenees. . . .

Hemingway's careful contrast of emotional and social climates makes the prefatory quotation from Ecclesiastes directly relevant. "One generation passeth away," says the preacher, "and another generation cometh; but the earth abideth forever." Wherever they go, Brett and her little coterie (the truly "lost" part of that otherwise unlost generation) carry along with them the neuroses of Montparnasse. But the earth fortunately abides. The sun rises and sets over the fields and woods of France and Spain. The fresh winds blow; the rivers run in the valleys; the white roads ascend the mountains. For those who will look at it, all this is available. But the wastelanders pass away and out of the picture, and there is no health in them.

This pleasurable contrapuntal method, with its subtly marked contrast of emotional and moral climates, continues into the climactic phase of the novel. Now, however, there is a new image to take the place of Burguete. When the Pamplona fiesta begins, the light (and the lightheartedness) which the fishermen have known in the Pyrenees grows dim and comes very near to going out. All the sullen jealousies and cross-purposes which Brett's presence causes are released among the vacationers. Outward signs of the venom which works within are Jake's obvious disgust at Cohn's fawning over Brett; Mike's relentless verbal bludgeoning of Cohn; and Cohn's physical bludgeoning of Mike and Jake. As if Brett's own neurosis were somehow communicable, her semi-voluntary victims writhe and snarl. All is vanity at Pamplona as it was in the Montparnasse cafés before the trip was undertaken.

For the Pamplona episodes the contrasting bright metal is not nature but rather a natural man, the brave matador Romero. He is used as a force of antithesis, manly, incorruptible, healthy, courageous, of complete integrity and self-possession. Beside him Mike seems a poor player indeed, and he conspicuously embodies the qualities which Cohn lacks. His control accents Cohn's emotionalism; his courage, Cohn's essential cowardice; his self-reliance, Cohn's miserable fawning dependence; his dignity Cohn's self-pity; his natural courtesy, Cohn's basic rudeness and egotism.

The enmity between the bullfighter and the boxer—for the very nature of Romero abhors the moral vacuum in Cohn—reaches its climax when Cohn invades Romero's room and finds Brett there. In a bedroom fist-fight the boxer has every advantage over the bullfighter except in those internal qualities which fists cannot touch. Though he is knocked down fifteen times, Romero will not lose consciousness, give up, shake hands, or stop trying to hit Cohn for as long as he can see him. Afterwards, like a Greek chorus, Bill and Mike close the chronicle-history of Robert Cohn, the pomaded sulker in the tent, and Romero, the manly and unspoiled warrior. "That's quite a kid," says Bill. "He ruined Cohn," says Mike. Cohn presently leaves Pamplona under the cloud of his own ruination. Romero's face may be cut up, but his moral qualities have triumphed, as they do again in the bullring the day following the brawl. He has been "beat-up" like many other members of his generation. But not "lost."

Maxwell Perkins, a good and perceptive editor, understood the intent of the novel perfectly. He admiringly called it "a healthy book, with marked satirical implications upon novels which are not—sentimentalized, subjective novels, marked by sloppy hazy thought." Its morality, like its esthetics, was notably healthy. Against the background of international self-seekers like Cohn, the true moral norm of the book (Bill and Jake at Burguete, Romero at Pamplona) stood out in high and shining relief.

Circe and Company

Hemingway's first novel provides an important insight into the special "mythological" methods which he was to employ with increasing assurance and success in the rest of his major writing. It is necessary to distinguish Hemingway's method from such "mythologizing" as that of [James] Joyce in *Ulysses*, or [T.S.] Eliot in *The Waste Land*. For Hemingway early devised and subsequently developed a mythologizing tendency of his own which does not depend on antecedent literatures, learned footnotes, or the recognition of spot passages. *The Sun Also Rises* is a first case in point.

It might be jocularly argued, for example, that there is much more to the portrait of Lady Brett Ashley than meets the non-Homeric eye. It is very pleasant to think of the Pallas Athene [the goddess Athena], sitting among the statuary in one of her temples like Gertrude Stein among the Picassos in the rue de Fleurus, and murmuring to the Achaeans, homeward bound from the battle of Troy: "You are all a lost generation." As for Brett, Robert Cohn calls her Circe [after the mythological sorceress]. "He claims she turns men into swine," says Mike Campbell. "Damn good. I wish I were one of these literary chaps." If Hemingway had been writing about brilliant literary chaps in the manner, say, of Aldous Huxley in *Chrome Yellow*, he might have undertaken to develop Cohn's parallel. It would not have been farther-fetched than Joyce's use of the Daedalus legend in *A Portrait of the Artist [as a Young Man]* or Eliot's kidnapping of Homeric Tiresias to watch over the mean little seductions of *The Waste Land*.

Was not Brett Ashley, on her low-lying island in the Seine, just such a fascinating peril as Circe on [the island of] Aeaea?

Did she not open her doors to all the modern Achaean chaps? When they drank her special potion of French applejack or Spanish wine, did they not become as swine, or in the modern idiom, wolves? Did not Jake Barnes, that wily Odysseus, resist the shameful doom which befell certain of his less wary comrades who became snarling beasts?

Without apology or explanation, Jake Barnes is a religious man. As a professing Catholic, he attends masses at the cathedral before and during fiesta week. On the Saturday before the festival opens. Brett accompanies him. "She said she wanted to hear me go to confession," says Jake, "but I told her that not only was it impossible but it was not as interesting as it sounded, and, besides, it would be in a language she did not know." Jake's remark can be taken doubly. The language Brett does not know is Latin; it is also Spanish; but it is especially the language of the Christian religion. When she goes soon afterwards to have her fortune told at a gypsy camp, Brett presumably hears language that she *can* understand.

Her true symbolic colors are broken out on Sunday afternoon. She is in the streets with Jake watching the religious procession in which the image of San Fermin is translated from one church to another. Ahead of the formal procession and behind it are the *riau-riau* dancers. When Jake and Brett try to enter the chapel they are stopped at the door, ostensibly because she has no hat [which at the time was mandatory for women inside Catholic churches]. But for one sufficiently awake to the ulterior meaning of the incident it strikingly resembles the attempt of a witch to gain entry into a Christian sanctum. Brett's witch-hood is immediately underscored. Back in the street she is encircled by the chanting pagan dancers who prevent her from joining their figure: "They wanted her as an image to dance around." When the song ends, she is rushed to a wineshop and seated on an up-ended wine-cask. The shop is dark and full of men singing,—"hard-voiced singing."

The intent of this episode is quite plain. Brett would not understand the language used in Christian confessional. She is forbidden to follow the religious procession into the chapel. The dancers adopt her as a pagan image. She is perfectly at home on the wine-cask amidst the hard-voiced singing of the non-religious celebrants. Later in fiesta week the point is re-emphasized. Jake and Brett enter the San Fermin chapel so that Brett can pray for Romero's success in the final bullfight of the celebration. "After a little," says Jake, "I felt Brett stiffen beside me, and saw she was looking straight ahead." Outside the chapel Brett explains what Jake has already guessed: "I'm damned bad for a religious atmosphere. I've got the wrong type of face."

She has, indeed. Her face belongs in wide-eyed concentration over the Tarot pack of Madame Sosostris, or any equivalent soothsayer in the gypsy camp outside Pamplona. It is perfectly at home in the center of the knot of dancers in the street or in the tavern gloom above the wine-cask. For Brett in her own way is a lamia [a female demon] with a British accent, a Morgan le Fay [King Arthur's legendary nemesis] of Paris and Pamplona, the reigning queen of a paganized wasteland with a wounded fisher-king as her half-cynical squire. She is, rolled into one, the *femme fatale de trente ans damnée* [seductress damned for thirty years]. Yet she is always and conspicuously herself. The other designations are purely arbitrary labels which could be multiplied as long as one's list of enchantresses could be made to last. They are not necessary to the full symbolic meaning which Brett has in her own right and by virtue (if that is the word) of what she is made to do in the book.

The "Lost Generation" Is Not All Lost

Although Hemingway carefully skirts the moralistic, as his artistic beliefs require, the moral drift of the symbolic story is unmistakable. Shortly after *The Sun Also Rises* appeared, he remarked, as he had never overtly done in the book, that "people aren't all as bad as some writers find them or as hollowed out and exhausted emotionally as some of the *Sun* generation." The restriction was conspicuous. He did not say, "the lost generation." He said rather, "some of the *Sun* generation." His indictment, put into dramatic terms, was directed against those who allowed themselves to flounder in an emulsion of ennui and alcohol when there was so much else to be done, whether one was a championship-winning *gueule cassée* [broken mouth] like Criqui or an ordinary citizen like Jake, engaged in readjusting himself to peace-time living. In contrast to the "hollow men" who went off the stage with something resembling a whimper, Hemingway presented another set of men who kept their mouths shut and took life as it came.

The emotional exhaustion of "some of the *Sun* generation" is accentuated by the oppositions Hemingway provides. Obviously no accidental intruder in the book is Romero, standing out in youthful dignity and strength against the background of displaced wastrels among whom Jake moves. The same is true of the interlude at Burguete, with Jake and Bill happily disentangled from the wastelanders, as if in wordless echo of Eliot's line: "In the mountains, there you feel free." However fascinating Brett and Cohn and Mike may be as free-wheeling international adventurers, the book's implicit attitude is one of quizzical condemnation towards these and all their kind.

Despite this fact, one finds in the presentation of Brett Ashley an almost Jamesian [reminiscent of Henry James] ambiguity. It is as if the objective view of Brett were intentionally relieved by that kind of chivalry which is never wholly missing from the work of Hemingway. On the straight narrative plane the book appears to offer a study of a war-frustrated love affair between Brett and Jake. Brett's Circean characteristics are only partly responsible for the sympathy with which she is treated, though all enchantresses from [Edmund] Spenser's

Acrasia to [Samuel Taylor] Coleridge's Geraldine are literally fascinating and Brett is no exception. Whenever Jake takes a long objective view of Lady Ashley, however, he is too honest not to see her for what she objectively is, an alcoholic nymphomaniac. To Cohn's prying questions about her, early in the book, Jake flatly answers: "She's a drunk."

There is, nevertheless, a short history behind her alcoholism and her constant restless shifting from male to male. During the war she was an assistant nurse; her own true love died; she married a psychotic British baronet who maltreated her; and at the time of the book she is waiting for a divorce decree in order to marry the playboy Mike Campbell. Furthermore—and this fact calls forth whatever chivalry one finds—she is in love with Jake, though both of them realize the hopelessness of the situation. She has not, as her fiancé observes, had an absolutely happy life, and Jake is prepared to take this into account when he judges her character. "Don't you know about Irony and Pity?" asks Bill Gorton during a verbal bout at Burguete. Jake knows all about them. They are the combination he uses whenever he thinks about Brett.

One of the ironies in the portrait of Brett is her ability to appreciate quality in the circle of her admirers. After the trip to San Sebastian with Robert Cohn she quickly rejects him. She does not do so sluttishly, merely in order to take up with another man, but rather for what to her is the moral reason that he is unmanly. Towards her fiancé Mike Campbell the attitude is somewhere in the middle ground of amused acceptance. He is Brett's sort, a good drinking companion living on an income nearly sufficient to allow him a perpetual holiday. "He's so damned nice and he's so awful," says Brett. "He's my sort of thing." Even though Brett can be both nice and awful with her special brand of ambiguity, she does save her unambiguous reverence for two men. One is the truly masculine Jake, whose total sexual disability has not destroyed his manhood. The other is Romero, whose sexual ability is obviously a recommendation but is by no means his only claim to admiration. It is finally to Brett's credit, and the measure of her appreciation of quality, that she sends Romero back to the bullring instead of destroying him as she might have done. This is no *belle dame sans merci* [beautiful lady without mercy]. She shows mercy both to her victim and to the remaining shreds of her self-respect.

The Heloisa-Abelard [tragic love] relationship of Brett and Jake is Hemingway's earliest engagement of an ancient formula—the sacrifice of Venus on the altar of Mars. In one way or another, the tragic fact of war or the after-effects of social disruption tend to inhibit and betray the normal course of love, not only in *The Sun Also Rises* but also in *A Farewell to Arms, To Have and Have Not, The Fifth Column, For Whom the Bell Tolls,* and *Across the River and Into the Trees.* Brett, the first of the victims, is a kind of dark Venus. If she had not lost her "true love" in the late war, or if Jake's wound had not permanently destroyed his ability to replace the lost lover, Brett's progressive self-destruction would not have become the inevitable course it now appears to be.

The Battle Between Health and Sickness

Much of the continuing power of *The Sun Also Rises* comes from its sturdy moral backbone. The portraits of Brett Ashley and Robert Cohn, like that of their antithesis Romero, are fully and memorably drawn. A further and deep-lying cause of the novel's solidity is the subtle operative contrast between vanity and sanity, between paganism and orthodoxy, between the health and humor of Burguete and the sick neuroses of the Montparnassian ne'er-do-wells. Other readers can value the book for the still-fresh representation of "the way it was" in Paris and Pamplona, Bayonne and Burguete, during the now nostalgically remembered middle Twenties. Yet much of the final strength of *The Sun Also Rises* may be attributed to the complicated interplay between the two points of view which it embodies. According to one of them, the novel is a romantic study in sexual and ultimately in spiritual frustration. Beside this more or less orthodox view, however, must be placed the idea that it is a qualitative study of varying degrees of physical and spiritual manhood, projected against a background of ennui and emotional exhaustion which is everywhere implicitly condemned.

Hemingway Challenges the Heroic "Code" in *The Sun Also Rises*

Arnold E. Davidson and Cathy N. Davidson

In their reading of The Sun Also Rises, *Arnold E. Davidson and Cathy N. Davidson find both Jake Barnes and Ernest Hemingway in violation of "the code" by which a true Hemingway hero lives. The Hemingway code was first written about by critic Philip Young, who identified the code hero as the man who, though wounded by events, manages to live an honorable life in which his actions speak louder than his words. The Davidsons argue that* The Sun Also Rises *is actually a devastating critique of the code of machismo. They interpret six passages to demonstrate that each time a character rises to heroism, Hemingway introduces a counterpoint of defeat into the text. Since each of these six passages presents gender ambiguously, the authors contend that Hemingway is challenging traditional gender roles. To understand the book, they urge the reader to reflect on the title. The sun will rise and set, and only the earth, and not heroes, will abide forever. Therefore, the abiding Earth, not any character, is the true hero of the novel. Cathy N. Davidson is the Ruth F. Devarney Professor of English at Duke University, and Arnold E. Davidson was a professor of English at Elmhurst College. Both authors have written extensively on modern literature and coauthored* The Art of Margaret Atwood.

[M]uch] of the criticism of [*The Sun Also Rises*] represents an attempt to determine "the code" governing its hero. And then, going beyond this first code, critics have

Arnold E. Davidson and Cathy N. Davidson, "Decoding the Hemingway Hero in *The Sun Also Rises*," in *New Essays on* The Sun Also Rises, edited by Linda Wagner-Martin, New York: Cambridge University Press, 1987, pp. 83–107. Copyright © Cambridge University Press 1987. Reprinted with the permission of Cambridge University Press.

searched for the code of all Hemingway heroes, Hemingway fictions, and, beyond that, have also postulated connections between the code meaning of the fiction, Hemingway's famous laconic prose style, and the author's life. But such a totalizing reading must somehow blink at its own inconsistencies. Jake, for example, clearly violates the code that, in the novel, most distinguishes him. His vaunted *afición* for the bullfight ends with his failure in that service. And if we attempt to equate the Hemingway hero with Hemingway himself as hero—soldier, war correspondent, hunter, bare-chested boxer, and so forth—that equation stumbles over the pose implicit in the strained tone with which the personal assertions are typically advanced. A true Hemingway hero would never be guilty of Hemingway's persistent claims to herohood. . . .

[We] will concern ourselves mainly with passages in which questions of gender and value judgments associated with gender are central. Ranging these fragments and their implications oppositionally against one another, we propose to indicate how the novel sets forth at one and the same time a pervasive coding and decoding of heroic (read: prototypically male) behavior.

> Two taxis were coming down the steep street. . . . A crowd of young men, some in jerseys and some in their shirtsleeves, got out. I could see their hands and newly washed, wavy hair in the light from the door. The policeman standing by the door looked at me and smiled. They came in. As they went in, under the light I saw white hands; wavy hair, white faces, grimacing, gesturing, talking. With them was Brett. She looked very lovely and she was very much with them.

This early passage carries particular narrative weight in that it marks the first entrance of Brett into the action of the novel and is itself marked, a few sentences later, by a loaded repetition: "And with them was Brett." Yet it is not Brett who elicits Jake's obvious and immediate reaction: "I was very angry. Somehow they always made me angry. I know they are supposed to be amusing, and you should be tolerant, but I wanted to swing on one, any one, anything to shatter that superior, simpering composure." We have here Brett, marked as desirable, set both with and against her companions, who are defined as objects of contempt, derision, and even a smoldering will to violence. But why is Jake so angry? In other words, how do we read his reading of these other men?

To begin with, we can supply the label that Jake (or Hemingway) declines to use. Consistent with the conventions of conversation and censorship of the time, the term "homosexual" remains, so to speak, in the closet. . . . Jake may be ill-equipped to deal with Brett's sexuality, but not from lack of desire. Lacking such desire, the gay young men who accompany Brett are thus defined as other—not men, not Jake.

The series of signs whereby this negative definition is communicated to the reader is itself highly revealing. We can first infer something of the suspect status of these others from the smile shared by Jake and the attending policeman (policemen, of course, are never wrong in such matters and are never homosexuals themselves). The smile, in short, is itself a code—a secret sign designed to affirm a bond of "true manhood" between Jake and the policeman, and that secret sign is itself underwritten by a more public one, the professional status of the policeman, whose smile carries quite another message than would a similar smile served up under the same circumstances by, say, the women's washroom attendant. . . .

The episode with the homosexuals functions . . . to reveal the contradictions in Jake's own life. His anger, his seemingly absolute dismissal of these men, may well result less from difference than from similarity. Jake relies upon their homosexuality to define his manhood (at least his desire is in the right place), but that definition is tested even as it is formulated by the joint presence of [the prostitute] Georgette and Brett. With either woman Jake does not perform, and must gloss over that fact with strained and painful explanation. Furthermore, if encounters with women who expect sexual attention regularly conduce to failure and frustration, no wonder that Jake, for most of the novel, prefers the company of men and finds a day on the river with Bill more satisfying than a night on the town with Brett. But where does that leave Jake, the unmanned manly "man without women"? The terrifying ambiguity of his own sexual limitations and gender preferences may well be one source of his anger (it usually is) with Brett's companions, and another reason why he articulates his anger and hatred for them before he reveals his love for her.

Membership in "Club Afición"

> When they saw that I had aficion, and there was no password, no set questions that could bring it out, rather it was a sort of oral spiritual examination with the questions always a little on the defensive and never apparent, there was this same embarrassed putting the hand on the shoulder, or a "Buen hombre." But nearly always there was the actual touching. It seemed as though they wanted to touch you to make it certain.

As in the first fragment where Jake and the policeman exchange a silent sign of their shared sexual identity, the men here again secretly, silently, jointly proclaim just who and what they are. But this passage effectively reverses the other in that now it is Jake who lacks authority, who must be judged. Moreover, like Jake with the homosexuals, the aficionados assess, without possibility of appeal, all men (women cannot even be included in the system of exclusion) who express an interest in bullfighting. Theirs is the perfect closed system: One either is in or one is not, it takes one to know one, and if you have to ask how you clearly do not belong. The very arbitrariness of the unspecified signs affirms their absolute significance. They can, indeed, outweigh other more obvious signs. The aficionados, for example, even touch in a kind of love, but with no hint of homosexuality.

Jake seems particularly proud of his membership in what might well be termed "Club Afición." Inclusion in such select groupings typically confers status and guarantees "character" even in the absence of any substantial corroborating evidence such as the large balance in one's bank account or the glowing testimony of one's associates—even in the presence of substantial evidence perhaps pointing in quite another and negative direction. . . .

But there is finally something suspect in the aficionados vesting so much of their own manhood in a boylike matador who, through girlish flirtation and enticement, woos a bull to its death. Restrained as their promotion is, these gentle men do protest too much, and the chief proof of that protest is their sustained but covert enterprise of interpretation whereby one sign must be translated into another. Thus the bullfighter's victory becomes the aficionados' victory; his triumph in the ring attests to theirs out of it despite the fact that Romero himself does not fare particularly well outside the ring, as indicated by his fight with Cohn (another defeat turned into victory) or his failed affair with Brett. For the aficionados, however, an artificial bestowing of death tokens a natural mastery over life, and, finally and fundamentally, the phallic trappings of the whole ceremony demonstrate the power and presence of the essential figurative and literal phallus that all "real men" share. . . .

Sexual Imagery and Bullfighting

Romero had the old thing, the holding of his purity of line through the maximum of exposure, while he dominated the bull by making him realize he was unattainable.

Romero smiled. The bull wanted it again, and Romero's cape filled again, this time on the other side. Each time he let the bull pass so close that the man and the bull and the cape that filled and pivoted ahead of the bull were all one sharply etched mass. It was all so slow and so controlled. It was as though he were rocking the bull to sleep.

For just an instant he and the bull were one.

He became one with the bull.

Immediately before Jake introduces Brett to Pedro Romero, Mike Campbell, her betrothed, shouts out in drunken isolence, "bulls have no balls," a phrase he twice repeats as Brett and Romero exchange their first faltering words, their long, longing glances. Campbell's code is easy to crack. His words only lightly disguise what he fears. As the preceding passages suggest, bulls, above all, in the symbol system of *afición* are defined by their difference from steers. Mike's body taunt readily translates, "bull's *are* balls, cojones." And so, as Mike also realizes full well are bullfighters: "Tell him Brett is dying to know how he can get into those pants," Mike shouts again, meaning, of course, that she is dying to know how she can. The covert sexuality in opposition to the imperatives of bullfighting soon becomes more obvious. Montoya subsequently sees Romero, "a big glass of cognac in his hand, sitting laughing between [Jake] and a woman with bare shoulders, at a table full of drunks. He did not even nod."

Once more the sexual imagery encoded in the text resonates in odd and contradictory ways with other images established in the book. Bulls and bullfighters are defined by their sexuality only when they abstain, only when they flirt with the opposite of sexuality, death. For example, immediately after Romero kills his last bull (the bull with which he was "one"), the boys run "from all parts of the arena" and "dance around the bull"—just as the homosexual men in the first passage discussed danced around Georgette, just as the Spanish men danced around Brett. The dead bull stands in for a living woman in this August fiesta in Pamplona, which itself reenacts an ancient fertility drama. But this is a peculiar drama in which males take all the parts—seducer seduced, actor/observer, animal/human, male/female. The bullfighter's conquest over the ultimately compliant and submissive bull is,

Hemingway's passion for bullfighting is reflected in The Sun Also Rises. *Here he is seen with renowned Spanish matador Antonio Ordonez in 1960.* Loomis Dean/Time and Life Pictures/Getty Images.

consequently, totally self-referential: the male as signifier and signified, the male as object and subject of his own desire.

Within the context of the ritual, that desire is not for fulfillment but for death. The final erotic embrace of man and beast is an embrace of annihilation. Not only have male and female been elided in this ritual, but sex (life) and death are also hopelessly intermingled. So replete are the sexual innuendoes in the passages describing Romero's conquest of his dark alter ego within the bullring that we are tempted to ask the question (perhaps in a different spirit than Hemingway intended): "Did the earth move for you, too, Pedro?" . . .

Pedro Romero exists not as a person for the aficionados but as an icon of essential masculinity. When Jake introduces Brett to Romero, he commits the ultimate iconoclasm by transforming Romero from transcendent symbol into a particular person and the subject, furthermore, of Brett's concrete and manifest sexual desire. Jake confuses the symbol with the substance, the icon with the man, and thus offends against not only the code of bullfighting but the whole concept of a code itself. He permits a literalization of spirituality, a degradation of an inviolable code to a set of odd and not particularly significant beliefs. By reducing the code hero, Romero, to a mere individual, a man with human sexual appetites, Jake irrevocably cancels his membership in the club and challenges the very code by which the club and the bullfight exist.

That challenge brings us finally to a question hidden by the text but on which the text turns. . . .

[Specifically], when the novel centers on the killing ground of the bullring and the paramount significance of all that transpires there, one can be led to wonder why the death of an animal is supposedly so much more meaningful than the death of a man. Or is it?

A Character's Death Casts a Shadow

> Later in the day we learned that the man who was killed was named Vicente Girones, and came from near Tafalla. The next day in the paper we read that he was twenty-eight years old, and had a farm, a wife, and two children. He had continued to come to the fiesta each year after he was married. The next day his wife came in from Tafalla to be with the body. . . . The coffin was loaded into the baggage-car of the train, and the widow and the two children rode, sitting, all three together, in an open third-class railway-carriage. The train started with a jerk, and then ran smoothly, going down grade around the edge of the plateau and out into the fields of grain that blew in the wind on the plain on the way to Tafalla. . . .

The anonymous man, the sudden senseless violent death, the mud—these signs suggest that Vicente Girones's demise is significant in its utter meaninglessness. That suggestion also carries over to the surrounding episodes, to Cohn's previous assault on Jake followed by his attack on Romero, to the subsequent bloody events in the bullring. Cohn has just spurned the role of the spurned lover to fight for Brett "like a man," so presently Romero although badly bruised, must still confront the "bull who killed Vicente Girones." The first privileged male violence might seem a little dubious, yet is it not redeemed by the second, which is itself magnified by the first? Romero's victory is all the greater because of his injury. But between these two interconnected actions falls the shadow of Girones's death, and that shadow effectively darkens the whole myth of chivalry and the excess of romanticism at the base of both episodes. More to the point, the death of Girones deflates all the rituals of violence. "All for fun. Just for fun," as the waiter testifies. Cohn thrashes Romero; the bull kills Girones; Romero kills the bull; and Brett simply forgets the bull's ear—the trophy, the final empty sign of all this valor—when she leaves town with Romero, an act (his, not hers) that, according to the same code that earlier signified his status as hero, now signifies he is not a true bullfighter. So much for the code. So much for the code hero. . . .

The fate and fact of Vicente Girones, however, brings symbolic death into fatal conjunction with the real thing. "You hear?" the waiter says to Jake. "Muerto. Dead. He's dead, with a horn through him. All for morning fun." The repetition of the word "dead," translated from one language to another to emphasize its finality in both, undercuts the ritual at the heart of the code, at the heart of the novel. A man dies so that a bull's ear can be cut off and given to a woman who leaves it in a bed table drawer along with some cigarette butts. What we have here is a devastating critique of the code. Even though the aficionados forget the lesson—Jake too, Jake most of all—in the excitement of the bullfight, the novel still insists that the other side and the underside of the ritual slaughter of the animal is pointless, quotidian human death and that the ritual cannot outweigh or cancel out this other death.

It is finally the widow and children who are left to pay the price for Girones's play at bravery. . . .

The Code for a Woman

"He really wanted to marry me. So I couldn't go away from him, he said. He wanted to make it sure I could never go away from him. After I'd gotten more womanly, of course."

. . .

Like other seemingly key passages, this one finally admits mostly different entrances into the text. For example, in tone it seems almost a conclusion, and yet it nevertheless still taunts the reader with the very impossibility of at last conclusively accounting for the characters, the book, or the author. Brett admits that "it was rather a knock his being ashamed of me," a new experience for her, obviously, not to be the object of unqualified male adoration. Does she send Romero away to avoid his judgment of her or to avoid having to accommodate herself to his rigorous (or unreasonable) standards? To avoid corrupting him or to save herself or to preserve safely in memory at least one glorious relationship? Hemingway does not resolve such questions; instead he equates them to similar parallel considerations such as the problematics of Romero's heroism or Jake's. For Brett too has been an icon for most of the novel, the unquestioned/unquestionable object of Jake's unfulfillable love, the motive for his abandonment of *afición*, of the code. Was it worth it? Does love conquer all and make everything all right, settle all doubts, resolve all ambiguities? Obviously not. Brett as icon is no more stable than Romero or Jake, and the code of self-fulfilling romantic love is every bit as undercut in the novel as the code of heroic solitary self-hood. And neither can the two codes inhabit the same novel. Thus Brett's most triumphant moment by virtue of one code "I'm thirty-four, you know. I'm not going to be these bitches that ruins children" is also, not coincidentally, her greatest defeat by virtue of the offset. The code for a woman, although only tangentially considered in this very masculine novel, is, it seems, as arbitrary, inconsistent, and contradictory as the code for a man.

The Meaning of the Final Passage

"Oh, Jake," Brett said, "we could have had such a damned good time together."

Ahead was a mounted policeman in khaki directing traffic. He raised his baton. The car slowed suddenly pressing Brett against me.

"Yes," I said. "Isn't it pretty to think so?"

THE END

Critics have tended to read the last line of the novel as Jake's redeeming realization of just where he stands and as a concluding promise, premised on that present awareness, of muted happiness in the future for this enduring and finally honest maimed man. . . .

But Jake's last words, with the suspended "THE END," do not simply point to a different future beyond the text. Taken in context, they necessarily return us to the text itself and the possibility of having it all to do all over again. Once more a woman presses against him in the cab. The symbolic policeman is again present, and he isn't smiling this time.

That same final dichotomy can be argued in a different way. The promise implicit in Jake's final words is a matter of codes and tone. If Jake claims the awareness that the critics mostly allow him, he can do so only if his question is read as the right statement, a brave declaration of independence and not a pathetic complicity in pretense. That right reading, in turn, depends on the final elevation of the heroic code—or at least the machismo one. If it (heroism or machismo) is at last self-evidently valid and unassailably authentic, then Jake, maimed as he is and ambiguous as his final gesture of manhood might be, must still be read in the right way. A man has to do what a man has to do. But nothing in the novel gives governing status to that ostensibly governing code. Since exercise in heroism are all along entangled with countering exercises in self-defeat, since success requires failure and is in complicity with it, since manliness is defined in terms of womanliness and is inescapably tied to it across the not-dividing slash, why should things be any different at the end?

Far from establishing any concluding finality or promising a different future beyond the text, Jake's last words readily devolve into an endless series of counterstatements that continue the same discourse: "Isn't it pretty to think so"/"Isn't it pretty to think isn't it pretty to think so?" and on ad infinitum, with each term in the sequence an affirmation and a question, a proclamation and a pose, and with each term thrown into a different perspective by the next one in the series. Instead of some redeeming recognition on which Jake can take his last stand, we have, then, implicit in his closing words, / endlessly repeated, and that repetition must finally cancel even itself out, dissolving / to nothingness, to the blank that follows the conclusion of any text. Or put differently, the negation at the end of the novel returns us finally to the promise of its title. As much as the sun rises, the sun also sets, and only the earth—not heroes, not their successes or their failures—abideth forever. . . .

Any final meaning of *The Sun Also Rises*, hinges, as we nave noted, on something as undefined as the vocal inflection of the written word. Depending on how we read Jake's concluding sentence, we can have a sadder and wiser man or a man still hoping against hope that, in another time, another place, happiness might yet be possible. But the final sentence is less Jake's sentence—his fate—in that the reader's, and the final point is that, returning to the novel's title and the epigraph from Ecclesiastes, the sun *also* rises, the sun *also* sets, and in many of life's lesser and greater moments it's pretty to think, "Isn't it pretty to think so?", saved and condemned by the ambiguities, the merciful incompleteness of the codes that render life both tolerable and terrifying.

Manhood and Performance in *The Sun Also Rises*

Thomas Strychacz

Thomas Strychacz contends that in Ernest Hemingway's early work, his heroes seek to validate their male identity by performing in front of an audience. In The Sun Also Rises, *Jake Barnes's role is to be an observer—to the romantic activities of his friends and to the splendid heroics of Pedro Romero in the bullring. When Barnes is called upon to act, Strychacz explains, he fails to live up to the manly code. However, Strychacz points out that a deeper reading of the text shows that Hemingway found Romero's performance somewhat theatrical and suggests that he, too, is lacking as a heroic figure. Strychacz concludes that Hemingway is saying there is not much difference, in the end, between the macho hero and the weaker male. Strychacz is a professor of English at Mills College.*

Hemingway's biographers and critics have never doubted that his obsessions with male authority shaped both his writing career and life. An "incorrigible attention-getter and impresario of his need to be situated always centre-stage," [as A. Robert Lee wrote,] Hemingway has been seen by defenders and detractors alike as the quintessential *macho* writer. . . .

Few critics, though, have seen in Hemingway's early works the extent to which the act of performance before an audience constitutes male identity, and even fewer have considered the troubling implications of this. Arising out of an audience's empowering acts of watching, a protagonist's sense of self rests precariously upon the audience's decision to validate or reject his ritual gestures toward manhood. Mastery of the

Thomas Strychacz, "Dramatizations of Manhood in Hemingway's *In Our Time* and *The Sun Also Rises*," *American Literature*, vol. 61, no. 2, May 1989, pp. 245–60. Copyright © 1989 Duke University Press. All rights reserved. Used by permission of the publisher.

arena bestows power on him, failure invites humiliation: in either case the process implies a loss of authority to the audience. Performances of manhood imply a radical lack of self that must be constantly filled and refashioned "while the crowd hollered." . . .

The Peformance of Romero

[As an] observer-figure at places of ritual, Jake Barnes shares . . . the displacement of self into seeing. . . . If Jake's pilgrimage to sacred places wins spiritual peace, his psychological travail in the arenas where men demonstrate their potency is painful indeed. In particular, the key scenes where Pedro Romero performs in the bull ring before the eyes of Brett and Jake force a complete reconsideration of the usual claims about the moral, mythic, or spiritual significance of the ritual encounter, and about the psychic renewal Jake gains from it.

Watching Romero typifies Jake's role in this novel, which is firmly established as that of observer and sometimes seer. "I have a rotten habit of picturing the bedroom scenes of my friends," remarks Jake in the second chapter. His impatience has transformed his friends' acts into theater and himself into director: his visionary ability appears to be at once a product of and compensation for his inability to participate in his own bedroom scenes. In another sense, Jake's "rotten habit" corresponds to that passionate witnessing which is his aficion. They "saw that I had aficion," claims Jake of Montoya's friends, as if aficion is a matter of seeing true rather than of interrogation. Several other characters comment on Jake's perceptiveness. Romero remarks: "I like it very much that you like my work. . . . But you haven't seen it yet. To-morrow, if I get a good bull, I will try and show it to you." And when Jake advises Montoya (to the hotel keeper's pleasure) not to give Romero the invitation from the American ambassador, Montoya asks Jake three times to "look" for him. Cast as the archetypal observer by other men who accept his evaluations of their endeavors, Jake has managed to transform observation itself into a kind of powerful witnessing. The closing scenes at Pamplona, however, will show how flimsy his authority truly is.

Approved by the adoring crowd as well as by Jake's expert appraisal, Romero's victories in the bull ring after the beating by Cohn are not only the narrative conclusion of Book II; they become the focus of Jake's own attempts to redeem his impotence. Jake perceives Romero's painful trial in the ring as a testing and affirmation of the matador's spirit—and perhaps, since Jake is another survivor of Cohn's assaults, as a vicarious affirmation of his own spirit: "The fight with Cohn had not touched his spirit but his face had been smashed and his body hurt. He was wiping all that out now. Each thing that he did with this bull wiped that out a little cleaner." Romero's process of recuperation, to Jake, depends upon a complex relationship between being watched and disavowing the watching audience (Brett in particular).

For *Sun*, and for Hemingway's early work in general, interpretation of this passage is crucial: "Everything of which he could control the locality he did in front of her all that afternoon. Never once did he look up. He made it stronger that way, and did it for himself, too, as well as for her. Because he did not look up to ask if it pleased he did it all for himself inside, and it strengthened him, and yet he did it for her, too. But he did not do it for her at any loss to himself. He gained by it all through the afternoon." Jake's conundrum of profit and loss (if Romero did it "all" for himself, what could be left for Brett?) involves, once again, the matador's intimate relationship with his audience. Unlike the older matador Villalta, who played to the crowd, Romero "did not look up" and thus, according to Jake, "did it all for himself inside." Even at the end of the fight, when the crowd tries to raise him in triumph, this most reticent of actors tries to resist: "He did not want to be carried on people's shoulders." Yet by defying the

The 1957 film version of The Sun Also Rises *starred (left to right) Errol Flynn as Mike Campbell, Ava Gardner as Lady Brett Ashley, Tyrone Power as Jake Barnes, Mel Ferrer as Robert Cohn, and Eddie Albert as Bill Gorton.* The Kobal Collection. Reproduced by permission.

rules of performance in Hemingway's quintessential arena, Romero appears to Jake to increase the potency of his actions. . . .

Yet Romero's mode of asserting his manhood is far more self-consciously part of a "system of authority" than Jake perceives. All of Romero's actions, in fact, are unashamedly theatrical: he performs as close to Brett as possible; he follows the wishes of the audience when, with the second bull, "the crowd made him go on," and proceeds to give a complete exhibition of bullfighting. He also holds his posture as consciously as any actor: he "finished with a half-veronica that turned his back on the bull and came away toward the applause, his hand on his hip, his cape on his arm, and the bull watching his back going away." Romero dispenses with the audience only because the audience is there. He never once looks up because the arena supplies an audience that never looks down, celebrating his actions for him. At the dramatic climax of the fight, the presentation of the bull's ear to Brett takes on significance precisely because it happens before an audience. As Jake describes it, "He leaned up against the barrera and gave the ear to Brett. He nodded his head and smiled. The crowd were all about him. Brett held down the cape." The crowd here is not merely an element of the scene: it is "all about," the element that creates a scene, converting the act of giving into a ceremony and transforming these actors into celebrities.

Considering the subtle but insistent theatricality of Romero's performance, the motives behind Jake's assertion that he does it "all for himself inside" becomes more complex than critics have generally recognized. . . . Jake's role at the ringside is actually far more than that of spectator, student, and teacher. . . . Jake, in fact, represses the element of theatricality in Romero's actions because of his own failure, in crucial senses, to control the way he displays himself. A complete characterization of Jake, then, must include the dramas of humiliation in which he plays the lead role.

Jake Takes the Stage

The key scene where Jake tacitly pimps for Brett in the café quickly becomes, once more, a drama of evaluatory watching. Brett claims, "I can't look at him," but Romero (as his performance in the bull ring suggests) is eager to display himself, quickly inviting Brett to "look" and "see [the] bulls in my hand." As befits his active participation in bringing Romero and Brett together, however, it is Jake who finally stands center stage. On leaving the café, Jake notices that the "hard-eyed people at the bull-fighter table watched me go" and comments drily, "It was not pleasant." Several things are not pleasant for Jake here: the sense that Romero has usurped him sexually, the sense that he has betrayed his tough male role by pimping for Brett. Above all, it is not pleasant that his failures are played out before a crowd of aficionados that watches and judges him.

Jake's appreciation of Romero's disdain for the crowd takes on a richer significance in the context of his humiliating failure to dramatize himself successfully before the "hard-eyed people." In the café, for the first time in the novel, he inadvertently steps into the part hitherto enacted by [a character] like Romero . . . : a man dramatizing his manhood before other men. Jake not only fails in this tough male role, he also betrays, before his co-aficionados, his compensatory ability to watch and evaluate others' masculine behavior. Every potent action of Romero's in the bullring thus recalls a double failure on Jake's part. It is telling that he prefaces his account of Romero's victories in the ring with a long description of Belmonte, another man who "watched" Romero perform. Belmonte's motives are Jake's: both men have suffered the contempt of the crowd, and both jealously watch Romero enact what they will never again possess.

In [*The Sun Also Rises*], Hemingway returns almost obsessively to the arenas where, he suggests, men typically act out their drama of power and shame. Some of these characters (Romero, . . . Villalta) demonstrate the authority accruing to the successful self-dramatist. More often, exposure to the watching crowd brings humiliation: in crucial senses, Jake . . . [reaches] center stage only to display [his] inadequacy. Audiences may be disappointing . . . , but more importantly they function as legitimating agents for men's images of themselves. . . . Jake, witness *par excellence*, [cultivates] an impression of the detached, potent observer. Yet Jake's valorization of Romero clearly disguises his own complex feelings about his failures to dramatize himself; seeing for Jake is not an antidote for his sexual impotency but rather another facet of it.

Taking their cue from the ostentatious swagger of Hemingway's life, critics have rarely credited him with a complex view of manhood. The evidence of . . . *The Sun Also Rises*, however, suggests that his ambivalence about the way men fashion a powerful male identity has been little understood. Hemingway's work severely disables the myth of the autonomous male individual. Characters like . . . Romero are authoritative men; yet they derive their charisma from manipulating an audience which then participates in the establishment of their power. Though . . . Jake [looks] weak by contrast, the strategies by which [he seeks] power are the same. Performance itself does not guarantee manhood; but manhood does require successful performance. Fashioning manhood "while the crowd hollers" and looks on is the crucial drama men undertake in Hemingway's early work: the moment when his characters undergo their most intense experiences of authority or humiliation.

The Education of Jake Barnes

Sam S. Baskett

In the following viewpoint, Sam S. Baskett, a literary critic, argues that each of Brett's lovers in The Sun Also Rises *values Brett in proportion to the type of man he is, his view of life, and his own sense of self worth. He divides the six men into two categories. Bill Gorton, Count Mippipopolous, and Mike Campbell live life on the surface, and to them, Brett is simply an attractive woman they would like to possess. Pedro Romero, Robert Cohn, and Jake Barnes are more complex figures. Each is changed by his love for Brett. By the end of the novel, Baskett explains, Jake has learned from his three tutors—Gorton, Romero, and the matador Belmonte—and sets out as a writer to live a moral life.*

Given what has become the critical consensus that [*The Sun Also Rises*] somehow expresses the way it was in Hemingway's early time, there has been surprising disagreement about just what is revealed by the distinctly different experiences of Jake Barnes, Pedro Romero, Robert Cohn and Bill Gorton, each of whom has received consideration as the moral center of a work that has also often been read as having no moral center. These contradictory readings have not been easy to reconcile, supported as they largely are by seemingly convincing evidence. Yet the counterpointed experiences of the novel's principal characters do resolve into a clearly discernible moral pattern if they are brought into sharp "literary" and "historical" focus, a pattern that in part constructs the time's moral history as well as embodies it.

Brett Is the Unfathomable New Woman

This is to say that the several lovers of Lady Brett Ashley fix upon her as an uncertain image of great value: to paraphrase

Sam S. Baskett, "'An Image to Dance Around': Brett and Her Lovers in *The Sun Also Rises*," *The Centennial Review*, vol. 22, winter 1978, pp. 45–69. Reproduced by permission.

the Lady herself, she is sort of what they have instead of God. To their image of her they make such overtures as the time and their individual capacities permit, overtures recalling the question [poet Robert] Frost's oven bird "frames in all but words.... what to make of a diminished thing": for the value each affixed to Brett is a function of his value of himself and the life he is able to live. From these combined self definitions emerges the "meaning" of the novel....

Brett's complicated characterization is enigmatically voiced in both French and English by Jake's concierge: "that lady, that lady there is some one. An eccentric, perhaps, but quelqu'une, quelqu'une." Assuredly, Brett is "some one," in more than one language. As a type of the new woman of the 1920's, she radiates independence, intelligence and beauty. She sees through "rot," sharing with Jake a more profound appreciation of the "modern temper" than that of the other characters. Her appearance reflects the new idea of beauty, her short hair "brushed back like a boy's"—indeed, Jake claims proudly, "she started all that." In a striking image that suggests both her femininity and her impersonality, she is described as being "built with curves like the hull of a racing yacht, and you missed none of it with that wool jersey." Apparently her own woman, in only a few weeks she engages sexually with at least two men in addition to her fiancé. Under the gaiety of Mike's quip that their hotel is a brothel is the serious theme of Brett's debasement of sex. Half asleep, Jake can confuse her voice with that of Georgette, the *poule* [prostitute] he takes to dinner.

Yet in her feminine attractiveness, debased or otherwise, Brett remains essentially unfathomable, somehow apart, as Jake states expressly. She has a way of looking "that made you wonder whether she really saw out of her own eyes. They would look on and on after every one else's eyes in the world would have stopped looking." This is surely extraordinary seeing, both in relation to Brett and in relation to Jake as he sees

Brett seeing. Jake immediately adds the ordinary, human dimension, however, appearing to recognize that the powers he attributes to her are illusory: "She looked as though there were nothing on earth she would not look at like that, and really she was afraid of so many things." But Brett, even when she is most "afraid," at least until the final scenes, is principally a contained figure to whom her suitors react, rather than a human being whose motives are susceptible to psychological analysis, Brett's "mystical penumbra" is greatly intensified by a number of suggestions that she is more than "just personal," even to Jake, "my own true love. . . [my only] friend in the world." In a passage of over one hundred words excised from the manuscript, Jake makes this dimension of their "own true love" even more explicit in an aside to his reader, disclaiming any psychological understanding of Brett or of his unbelievable passion for this person who determines his world. Perhaps Hemingway felt that enough evidence of Brett's strangeness remained in the novel, for there are many motifs suggesting her uniqueness, even apart from her magnification by her different lovers. For example, ironically enough, her promiscuity, which seems almost maternal, never casually salacious. . . .

In another persistent motif, Brett seems to seek absolution for her actions through her compulsion to bathe, a persistence that expresses a desire for purification transcending cleanliness. But Brett's extraordinary dualities are most directly suggested in Pamplona, where on one occasion she walks through the crowd, "her head up, as though the fiesta were being staged in her honor". Earlier, on the afternoon of "the big religious Procession" when "San Fermin was *translated* from one church to another," Brett is stopped inside the church because she is hatless. Clearly she is the wrong image for the church, too much a disheveled Venus to be allowed in the presence of the Virgin. Even appropriately attired, "I'm damned bad for a religious atmosphere. . . . I've got the wrong type of face." Outside, however, in the street that runs

> from the chapel into town. . . lined on both sides with people keeping their place. . . for the return of the procession. . . dancers formed a circle around Brett and started to dance. . . . They took Bill and me by the arms and put us in the circle. Bill started to dance, too. They were all chanting. Brett wanted to dance but they did not want her to. *They wanted her as an image to dance around.* (italics added)

The interpretation is Jake's, of course, but Brett's actions here, as throughout much of the novel, indicate that, try as she will to be merely a dancer, she possesses an aspect, however "wrong," that causes her to be an image "translated" from one sort of "church" to another—the otherwise empty space between the "chapel" and "town" around which a number of people dance in the absence of the return of "the big religious procession."

Bill, the Count, Mike Have Shallow Relationships with Brett

Six men in *The Sun Also Rises* offer Brett such love as they have: Bill Gorton, Count Mippipopolous, Mike Campbell, Pedro Romero, Robert Cohn and Jake Barnes. The first three listed are without illusions. . . . To them, there is no supreme value and Brett, far from incarnating such an ideal, is a sexually tantalizing woman whom each in his own way wants to possess. It is easy to overlook the fact that at first Bill is much taken by her. Appreciative of the "Beautiful lady. . . . Going to kidnap us" before he has even met her, he responds to her spirited, openly flirtatious manner with a wittily veiled allusion to fornication and a promise to join her later. In only a few minutes, he has decided she is "Quite a girl," but on learning of her engagement to Mike he backs away, and there are no more charged exchanges, even rarely any conversation, between them. His immediate and total withdrawal expresses both his attitude toward Brett and his general approach to life. . . .

The count explains to Jake and Brett the "secret" of his enjoyment of life: "You must get to know the values." Having established his scheme in terms of what he can buy, he buys— champagne from his friend Baron Mumms, gourmet meals, a "houseful" of antiquities, eighteen-eleven brandy, ladies with "class." Later, praying to "make a lot of money," Jake is reminded of the count. When Brett amusedly queries whether love has any place in his values,—a question in itself emphasizing her role in the novel—he responds that he is always in love. "That, too, has got a place in my values." Brett retorts, "You're dead," for she well understands that place: ten thousand dollars if she will go to Biarritz with him. To the count— who never "joke[s] people. Joke people and you make enemies"—love is obviously a serious business; it is either purchasable or not. With his love, as with his wine, the count does not intend "to mix emotions up" lest he will "lose the taste." Despite his impressive wounds, the count is hardly the hero much critical commentary has made of him.

Like Bill and the count. Mike sets a high value on his fiancée's sexual attractiveness: she, to him, is "a lovely piece." His emotions, of course, are involved to an extent precluded by Bill's irony and the count's accountant practicality, but they arise from his need for a mutual dependence, rather than any commitment to ideal worth. As Mike writes to Jake, "I know her so well and try to look after her but it's not so easy." Nor is it easy for Brett to look after Mike, in his view the original basis of their relation: "she loves looking after people. That's how we came to go off together. She was looking after me." At the end, although she cannot bring herself to marry him, she plans to go back to Mike, and they doubtless will live in a brothel of sorts, alcohol and good-natured carelessness Mike's only defense against their mutual inadequacies in "looking after" each other.

Cohn Is Changed by Brett

Bill, the count and Mike remain unchanged by their "love" for Brett. Cohn, on the other hand, is vulnerable to passion and transformed by it. Boyishly cheerful, "he had been moulded by the two women who had trained him." His present "lady"—so designated four times in one page by Jake—had taken him in hand: "Cohn never had a chance of not being taken in hand. And he was sure he loved her." "[L]ed. . . quite a life" by this demanding mistress, he is also the servant of a romantic imagination, stimulated by his reading of "splendid imaginary amorous adventures. . . in an intensely romantic land"—as a guidebook to what life holds in Jake's appraisal, "about as safe as it would be. . . to enter Wall Street direct from a French convent, equipped with a complete set of the more practical Alger books." In this unique figure facetiously suggesting an "exchange" of financial and religious values, Jake dramatically presents Cohn's danger. . . .

Cohn is thus by temperament recklessly ready for "amorous adventures" of greater intensity than that afforded by his liaison with Frances, who, even though she is unaware of Brett, describes what Cohn is looking for.

> I know the real reason Robert won't marry me. . . . It's just come to me. They've sent it to me in a vision in the Cafe Select. Isn't it mystic? Some day they'll put a tablet up. Like at Lourdes. . . . Why, you see, Robert's always wanted to have a mistress. . . . And if he marries me. . .that would be the end of all the romance.

The "mystic" vision . . . is not Frances's, of course, but Cohn's; for from the first, he looks at Brett as Moses looked "at the promised land," a vision superseding his desire for romantic life in South America. He is ready to fight the next day when Jake calls her less than perfect. Cohn finds in her a certain indescribable "quality": "I shouldn't wonder if I were in love with her." Even in such a detail as his tennis game he is changed by his love. Formerly he had "loved to win"; now he doesn't care when "People beat him who had never had a chance with him." Faced with her profanation of what he regards as a sacramental union, he calls her Circe, but never denies her power over him, following her around "like a poor bloody steer," in Mike's drunken analogy. Cohn does not think of himself as a steer, however, and he ultimately does "battle for his lady love" until he is routed from the ambiguous world represented by Brett.

Concerned as he is with being a writer, Jake confesses in Chapter VI, to a difficulty in showing Cohn clearly, giving as the reason, "I never heard him make one remark that would, in any way, detach him from other people" until he fell in love with Brett. Again, "If he were in a crowd nothing he said stood out." Yet manifestly Cohn does stand out for Jake—he begins his novel with him, is concerned to show him clearly and comes to be "blind, unforgivingly jealous of what had happened to him." One explanation, beyond jealousy, for Jake's blindness toward Cohn is that in him he may well see himself, both in his hopeless love and in the attitudes that make him vulnerable to such a love. . . .

Romero Needs to Change Brett

Jake goes to the bull fights to see great matadors work "in the terrain of the bull" and thus to be given the traditional "tragic sensations" of pity and fear. What he must be struck by, however, is the pointed contrast with the way he had been living his life, in self pitying, futile aspiration, rather than "all the way up" as he had once characterized the life of the bull fighter to Cohn. "Everybody behaves badly," he tells Brett. "Given the proper chance, I'd be as big an ass as Cohn," and the "phantom suitcase" he now carries is part of his new recognition of himself in this light, in expecting from Brett, and from life, what he is not going to get. Romero, however, does not "behave badly" in or out of the ring, and as a bull fighter, through his "greatness" he enables his audience, including Jake, to experience the "sensations" of tragedy. Romero, in keeping with his name either as "pilgrim" or "pilot fish," provides Jake with a momentary vision of the stance he would like to be able to assume, not in the bull ring but in his entire life. In this sense Romero, in another dimension than Bill, serves as Jake's tutor.

But what of Romero outside the ring? There remains to consider him as Brett's lover. After saying that Romero had the "greatness," Jake adds, "he loved bull-fighting and I think he loved the bulls, and I think he loved Brett." Certainly he responds to Brett's encouragement, even though he has earlier been informed that Mike is doing "[n]othing. . . waiting to marry this lady." In contrast to Bill, he is undeterred by this information. And he performs for her in the bull ring, maneuvering the action in front of her, presenting her with the ear he is awarded for his triumph. But he is distinctly not a knight like Cohn, "ready to do battle for his lady love." His performance as a matador, as well as his fight with Cohn, is first of all for himself and only incidentally for Brett. He even has a bit of condescending humor as he presents the ear to her. "'Don't get bloody,' Romero said, and grinned." He defines himself not primarily as Brett's lover as do Cohn and Jake, but as a bull fighter, with no commitment of any sort between himself and his vocation. Jake makes the distinction: "He loved bull-fighting. . .and I think he loved Brett."

In what way does he love her? After "a final look to ask if it were understood," he proceeds sexually in accordance with that understanding. His initial tentativeness arises both from his natural disbelief that this woman from what must seem another world is available, and also from his youth. He is repeatedly designated a "lad," "boy," "kid," or "child" by Montoya, Jake and Brett. Montoya is particularly concerned with his immaturity outside the ring. "'Any foreigner' can flatter [a boy like that]." Learning that this nineteen-year-old primitive wanted to marry the thirty-four-year-old sophisticate, Jake summons enough humor to say. "Maybe he thought it would make him Lord Ashley." After Brett sends him away, she feels good at not ruining "children." And Romero, surely dimly understanding that he is out of his element, does go—back to his true love, bull fighting. He would have married her, Brett tells Jake, "to make it sure I could never go away from him," after she had grown her hair out and "gotten more womanly, of course." Romero, in his boyish self-confidence, wants Brett for his woman. He has only "been" with two before, Brett says, and until this experience "never cared about anything but bull-fighting." But he only wants to marry Brett if she will fit *his* naïve image of a wife, the wife of a matador committed to his vocation. We do not fully know Romero's story, of course, but there is nothing in what we do know to suggest that Brett determines his world in the way she does that of Cohn and Jake: she is not his goddess. It is as impossible to consider his momentary expression of youthful male ardor for a sexually exciting woman as committed love as it is to understand how he has been read as fully heroic. . . .

Jake Is Tested and Prevails

At the beginning [of *The Sun Also Rises*], Jake . . . is the tyro, but by the end he has learned much from three tutors, Bill, Romero, and Belmonte: from the negative examples of Cohn, Mike and the count; as well as from the head blows of Cohn, Brett's lover most like himself. The extent of his development, and its limitation, is apparent in the final scenes.

In Book III, which opens just after Jake's "world was not wheeling any more," it is "all over." Specifically, it is the fiesta that is finished, but more widely, it is the entire sequence of events that has wrought a change in Jake and his world, most particularly, his love of Brett. He says goodby to Bill in France, and Jake goes back to Spain, "recover[ing] an hour": they are in different countries and times. Jake proceeds steadily and quietly through the routine of his days in San Sebastian, seeming to gather strength from swimming in the "green and dark" water, from vistas of a "green mountainside" and "a green hill with a castle." Very explicitly, after Jake has filled out his "police bulletin" and is swimming in the sea, there is imagery of depth, anticipating the elevation of the Madrid scenes.

> Then I tried several *dives. I dove deep* once, swimming *down* to the *bottom.* I swam with my eyes open and it was green and *dark.* The raft [with two lovers on it] made a *dark shadow.* I came out of the water beside the raft, pulled up, *dove* once more, holding it for length, and then swam ashore. (italics added)

Both his state of mind and the natural scenery suggest something of the mood of the episode at Burguete, but there is a difference. In San Sebastian, he sustains himself, unsupported by Bill's noisy camaraderie, and he seems more in control of his universe.

This serenity is put to test when Brett summons him to Madrid. At first, he seems in danger of reverting to the self-pitying attitude of Paris:

> That seemed to handle it. That was it. Send a girl off with one man. Introduce her to another to go off with him. Now go and bring her back. And sign the wire with love. That was it all right.

Here again is the familiar tone of helpless, desperate commitment. Jake seems ready to resume his dance around Brett's image, transfixed in a desire that can neither be denied nor satisfied—in effect endowing Brett with a "mystical penumbra" and making his worship of her serve for his "big religious possession." Jake is different, however, as a careful reading makes clear. Brett is now reduced to "a girl" in difficulty, and "love" is a "sign." For better and worse, Jake is no longer dancing around Brett's image in quite the same measures. . . .

By the final scenes in Madrid, Jake is able to bold himself steady in the paradox of wanting everything and having nothing except himself—[poet] Emily Dickinson's paradox of "The Missing All"—both states expressed in his absurd, magnificent passion for Brett, and captured in his final words. He is not yet a tragic hero pushing resolutely toward a victory of spirit against the inevitable defeat of circumstance, but he is at his own "boundary situation." If he is not, like Santiago [in Hemingway's *Old Man and the Sea*], "beyond all the people in the world," he is farther out than he has been before. Much closer in time and situation to [Hemingway character] Nick Adams in "Big Two-Hearted River," who "wanted to be a great writer," he is not yet ready to fish "In the swamp [where]. . . the fishing would be tragic. In the swamp fishing was a tragic adventure. Nick did not want it." Neither does Jake seem to "want it" as he holds himself tautly against the pressures of his life in the final scenes of the novel.

But Jake obviously does "want it." His experiences do not end in Madrid, in the taxi with Brett. They end with his seeking out the meaning of his impossible/possible love for Brett through the writing of *The Sun Also Rises*. . . . In the process of writing the "poem" of his life, Jake composes, in effect, his "love song"—the uniqueness distinguishing his human syllable from that of Brett's other lovers whom he knows in secret kinship. Faced with playing things as they are, he finally neither asserts in foolish desperation as Cohn, nor abdicates his full human responsibility as do the other lovers in their separate ways. Rather as the artist he set out to "create in honesty" a world in which he can live as a moral being. Bill had taunted him at Burguete with not knowing irony and pity, "And you claim you want to be a writer, too. You're only a newspaper man. An expatriated newspaper man." Bill is a writer, and a successful one; but he limits himself to "travel stories" and "nature-writ[ing]." Tragedy is beyond his reach. Jake, however, will not accept such limitations. Unlike Bill, and Cohn, another writer of limited vision, he really is ultimately concerned with "an abnormal life," one lived "all the way up." *The Sun Also Rises* is a record of how he attempts to learn to live that life. Seeing all around him, as well as inside himself, evidences of the death of value, Jake chooses, even in recognition of that extinction, to create his own "All"—*The Sun Also Rises*—and in the act of so doing comes on a "moral history" that at once follows the pattern of the age but also deepens and enriches its tragic colors.

The Mythical Role of
Lady Brett Ashley

Leslie Fiedler

In this groundbreaking work, the author, a literary critic and professor, argues that American writers are incapable of dealing with adult sexuality and are pathologically obsessed with death. He finds Ernest Hemingway only really at ease when dealing with "men without women." Fiedler considers Hemingway's female characters to be generally two-dimensional. An exception is Lady Brett Ashley, whom he considers Hemingway's most "satisfactory" female character. However, she is presented as a "bitch-goddess," more a mythical figure than a real person.

Hemingway is only really comfortable in dealing with "men without women." The relations of father to son, of battle-companions, friends on a fishing trip, fellow inmates in a hospital, a couple of waiters preparing to close up shop, a bull-fighter and his manager, a boy and a gangster: these move him to simplicity and truth. Perhaps he is best of all with men who stand alone—in night-time scenes when the solitary individual sweats in his bed on the verge of nightmare, or arises to confront himself in the glass; though he is at home, too, with the Rip Van Winkle archetype, with men in flight from women. Certainly, he returns again and again to the fishing trip and the journey to the war—those two traditional evasions of domesticity and civil life. Yet he feels an obligation to introduce women into his more ambitious fictions, though he does not know what to do with them beyond taking them to bed. All his life, he has been haunted by a sense of how simple

Leslie Fiedler, from *Love and Death in the American Novel*, rev. ed. New York: Stein and Day, 1966, Dalkey Archives, 1997. Copyright © 1966, 1960 by Leslie A. Fiedler. All rights reserved. Reproduced by permission.

it all was once, when he could take his Indian girl into the clean-smelling woods, stretch out beside her on the pine-needles (her brother standing guard), and rise to no obligations at all. . . .

In Hemingway the rejection of the sentimental happy ending of marriage involves the acceptance of the sentimental happy beginning of innocent and inconsequential sex, and camouflages the rejection of maturity and of fatherhood itself. . . .

The Dark Lady and the Fair Lady

[The] fate in Hemingway's imagination of all Anglo-Saxon women [is to be a bitch]. In him, the cliché of Dark Lady and Fair survives, but stood on its head, exactly reversed. The Dark Lady, who is neither wife nor mother, blends with the image of Fayaway, the exotic servant-consort reconstructed by [Herman] Melville in *Typee* out of memories of an eight-year-old Polynesian girl-child. In Hemingway, such women are mindless, soft, subservient; painless devices for extracting seed without human engagement. The Fair Lady, on the other hand, who gets pregnant and wants a wedding, or uses her sexual allure to assert her power, is seen as a threat and a destroyer of men. But the seed-extractors are Indians or Latins, black-eyed and dusky in hue, while the castrators are at least Anglo-Saxon if not symbolically blond. Neither are permitted to be virgins; indeed, both are imagined as having been often possessed, though in the case of the Fair Woman promiscuity is used as a device for humiliating and unmanning the male foolish enough to have entered into a marriage with her. Through the Dark anti-virgin, on the other hand, a new lover enters into a blameless communion with the other uncommitted males who have possessed her and departed, as well as with those yet to come. It is a kind of homosexuality once-removed, the appeal of the whorehouse (Eden of the world of men without women) embodied in a single figure.

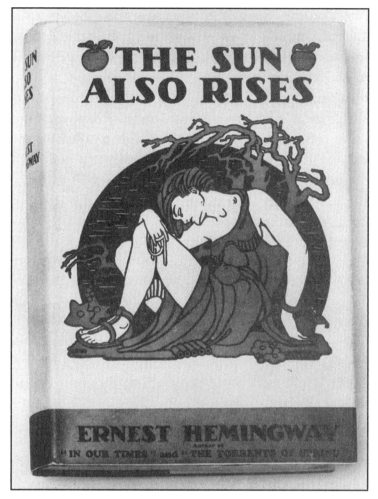

The first edition of The Sun Also Rises *was published in 1926.* Herbert Orth/ Time and Life Pictures/Getty Images.

When Hemingway's bitches are Americans, they are hopeless and unmitigated bitches. . . .

Brett as "Bitch-Goddess"

The British bitch is for Hemingway only a demi-bitch, however, as the English are only, as it were, demi-Americans. Catherine [in *A Farewell to Arms*] is delivered from her doom by death; Brett Ashley in *The Sun Also Rises* (1926) is permitted, once at least, the gesture of herself rejecting her mythical role. But it is quite a feat at that, and Brett cannot leave off congratulating herself: "You know it makes one feel rather good deciding not to be a bitch." Yet Brett never becomes a woman really; she is mythicized rather than redeemed. And if she is the most satisfactory female character in all of Hemingway, this is because for once she is presented not as an animal or as a nightmare but quite audaciously as a goddess, the bitch-goddess with a boyish bob (Hemingway is rather fond of women who seem as much boy as girl), the [evil spirit] Lilith of the '20's. No man embraces her without being in some sense castrated, except for Jake Barnes who is unmanned to begin with; no man approaches her without *wanting* to be castrated, except for Romero, who thinks naïvely that she is—or can easily become—a woman. Indeed, when Brett leaves that nineteen-year-old bullfighter, one suspects that, though she avows it is because she will not be "one of those bitches who ruins children," she is really running away because she thinks he might *make* her a woman. Certainly, Romero's insistence that she let her hair grow out has something to do with it: "He wanted me to grow my hair out. Me, with long hair. I'd look so like hell. . . . He said it would make me more womanly. I'd look a fright."

To yield up her cropped head would be to yield up her emancipation from female servitude, to become feminine rather than phallic; and this Brett cannot do. She thinks of herself as a flapper, though the word perhaps would not have occurred to her, as a member of the "Lost Generation"; but the Spaniards know her immediately as a terrible goddess, the avatar of an ancient archetype. She tries in vain to enter into the circle of Christian communion, but is always turned aside at the door; she changes her mind, she has forgotten her hat [a requirement for women inside Catholic churches at the time]—the apparent reason never matters; she belongs to a world alien and prior to that of the Christian churches in which Jake finds a kind of peace. In Pamplona, Brett is surrounded by a group of *riau-riau* dancers, who desert a religious procession to follow her, set her up as a rival to Saint Fermin: "Some dancers formed a circle around Brett and started to dance. They wore big wreaths of white garlic around their necks. . . . They were all chanting. Brett wanted to dance but they did not want her to. They wanted her as an image to dance around." Incapable of love except as a moment in bed, Brett can bestow on her worshipers nothing more than the brief joy of a drunken ecstasy—followed by suffering and deprivation and regret. In the end, not only are her physical lovers unmanned and degraded, but even Jake, who is her priest and is protected by his terrible wound, is humiliated. For her service is a betrayal not only of his Catholic faith but of his pure passion for bullfighting and trout-fishing; and the priest of the bitch-goddess is, on the purely human level, a pimp. . . .

An Earthly Paradise for Men Only

In America, the earthly paradise for men only is associated, for obvious historical reasons, with the "West"; and it is possible to regard the classic works [like *The Sun Also Rises*] in this sense, as "Westerns." Despite certain superficial differences, they are, indeed, all closely related to the pulp stories, the comic-books, movies, and TV shows, in which the cowhand and his side-kick ride in silent communion through a wilderness of sagebrush, rocks, and tumbleweed. The Western, understood in this way, does not even require an American setting, being reborn, for instance, in Hemingway's *The Sun Also Rises* in the improbable environs of Paris and Burguete. One must not be confused by the exotica of expatriation: bullfights, French whores, and *thés dansants* [tea dancing]. Like the American East, Paris in Hemingway's book stands for the world of women and work, for "civilization" with all its moral complexity, and it is presided over quite properly by the bitch-goddess Brett Ashley. The mountains of Spain, on the other hand, represent the West: a world of male companions and sport, an anti-civilization, simple and joyous, whose presiding genius is that scarcely articulate arch-buddy, "good, old Bill."

For Hemingway there are many Wests, from Switzerland to Africa; but the mountains of Spain are inextricably associated in his mind with the authentic American West, with Montana whose very name is the Spanish word for the mountains that make of both isolated fastnesses holy places. It is in the Hotel Montana that Lady Ashley ends up after her abortive romance with the bullfighter Romero; and it is from the University of Montana that Robert Jordan, hero of *For Whom the Bell Tolls*, takes off to the Spanish Civil War. But it is not only a pun that binds together for Hemingway his two paradisal retreats; it is also the sacred sport of fishing. Though the monastery of Roncesvalles stands on a peak high above Jake's place of refuge, it serves only to remind Hemingway's characters of a religion now lapsed for them. "It's a remarkable place," one of them says of the monastery; but Bill, the good companion, observes mournfully, "It isn't the same as fishing, is it?"

It is in the trout stream of Burguete that Jake and Bill immerse themselves and are made whole again and clean; for that stream links back to the rivers of Hemingway's youth, the rivers of upper Michigan, whose mythical source is the Mississippi of Tom Sawyer and Huck Finn. "We stayed five days at Burguete and had good fishing. The nights were cold and the days were hot. . . . It was hot enough so that it felt good to wade in the cold stream, and the sun dried you when you came out. . . ." They are boys again, back on Jackson's Island, which is to say, safe in the Neverland of men without women. Jake is, in his quest for the Great Good Place, at one with almost all the other heroes of Hemingway.

Lady Brett Ashley as the New Woman

Wendy Martin

The author, a professor of English at Claremont Graduate University and editor of Women's Studies, *examines shifting gender roles in* The Sun Also Rises. *Following the turmoil of World War I, Wendy Martin explains, prototypical woman was transformed from a homebound, obedient creature to an autonomous, educated individualist: in short, the New Woman of the Jazz Age. Lady Brett Ashley is representative of the New Woman, according to Martin, and her promiscuous relationships with men reflect the confusion of the post–World War I world. However, Brett remains caught between the role of the idealized woman and that of the modern woman. Together, Martin states, Brett and Jake reflect the shifting definitions of gender in the Jazz Age. As the novel plays out, Jake takes on more traditional female qualities, while Brett displays the bold assertive traits more often associated with men.*

The Sun Also Rises, published in the autumn of 1926, became, along with *The Great Gatsby* [written by F. Scott Fitzgerald], published the previous year, the novel that captured the excitement of the jazz age and expatriate glamour as well as the cultural dislocation and psychological malaise that were the legacy of World War I. The emotional upheavals of Jake Barnes and Brett Ashley, and their friends Bill Gorton, Mike Campbell, and Robert Cohn, who live episodically, taking risks and contending with the elation or despair that follows in the wake of their adventures, provide a cartography of the experience of the lost generation. In this novel filled with

Wendy Martin, "Brett Ashley as New Woman in *The Sun Also Rises*," *New Essays on* The Sun Also Rises, edited by Linda Wagner-Martin, New York: Cambridge University Press, 1987, pp. 65–82. Copyright © Cambridge University Press 1987. Reprinted with the permission of Cambridge University Press.

surface excitement—love, sexual rivalry, cafe hopping in France, the revelry of the festival of San Fermin in Pamplona, fishing excursions in the Spanish countryside—Brett and Jake emerge as the paradigmatic couple who best represent the shift in the perception of gender following World War I. This redefinition of masculinity and femininity was not an abrupt rift in the cultural landscape but rather a gradual shifting of the ground on which the edifice of Victorian sexual identity was built.

The blending of the polarized spheres that traditionally separated the lives of women and men was, in part, the result of the centrifugal swirl of events following World War I. . . .

In *The Sun Also Rises* Hemingway makes it clear that the postwar sensibility as exemplified by Jake is one of severe loss, emasculation, and impotence. In contrast to Robert Cohn's anachronistic readiness to fight to protect his honor or defend his lady from insults, Jake feels tricked by the war and is dismayed at having been a pawn in an international con game masterminded by bankers and politicians. . . .

Postwar Shifting of Gender Roles

With the loss of the conviction of masculine invincibility and authority after the war came a stoic attitude that is a compensatory stance for this new awareness of vulnerability. Hemingway's definition of courage, which he succinctly phrased as "grace under pressure," is in many respects a startling echo of the Victorian adage to "suffer and be still" that was directed to women who felt helpless to meet the demands of their sacrificial role. Just as the true woman was self-effacing in the name of familial and social stability, the ideal man of Hemingway's world consciously suppressed his feelings, thereby neutralizing his response in the name of courage or mastery and the need to protect his country. But the stoicism and willed mastery are seen as an obligation or a challenge to be met consciously rather than as a natural—that is to say, habitual—response. Certainly this form of willed courage is not glorious, nor is it even a prerogative; instead it is a necessity born out of the need to conceal masculine vulnerability and loss of certainty.

A further parallel between the psychic cost of the redemptive role of Victorian women and the disequilibrium of the war-weary man of the lost generation can be seen in the extreme in their respective pathologies—hysteria and shell shock. Both are somatic responses to psychological conflicts; hysteria is a female response to the inability to reconcile the need for self-expression and the cultural imperative for self-denial, and shell shock is a parallel response of men who are terrified of combat and death on the battlefield, Interestingly, hysteria is a response to excessive domestic *confinement* and shell shock to excessive *exposure*. Yet both of these extremes produce the same range of symptoms—including exhaustion, confusion, speech defects, blindness, deafness, and paralysis.

In the gap of meaning that opened after World I, the female role was undergoing a transformation in the popular consciousness from passive, private creature to avid individualist in pursuit of new experiences. The housebound Victorian nurturer was becoming the modern woman of unprecedented mobility and public visibility. Traditionally, women have inhabited private spaces, which are simultaneously protected and claustrophobic. Along with the opportunities created by the dissolution of polarized social spheres came increased vulnerability for women. Because public space is defined as male, women were often seen either as interlopers or as "fair game" undeserving of respect or safety. Frequently a woman who left the sanctity of the home was automatically defined as disreputable or dangerous.

Although the highly glamorized flapper seen dancing, smoking, and drinking in public and consorting with men of her own choice in cafés and dancehalls was largely a media phenomenon, the image of the short-skirted, shimmying, seductive, sleek femininity promised unprecedented freedom for twentieth-century women in general. Emphasis on mobility and active participation in public life for women in the 1920s—the first decade in which women had the vote—seemed to represent a dramatic break with the past; but in fact, the postwar decade actually consolidated the gains that had been achieved by feminists over a period of almost 100 years.

In the late nineteenth century the new woman, like the modern woman of the 1920s, was a product of the urban life of the developing industrial cities. She was educated, valued her autonomy, and did not automatically subscribe to the values of the family; frequently, she was single and had a career. No longer did she define herself as a domestic being; openly rebelling against nineteenth-century bourgeois priorities, the new woman rejected traditional feminine ideals of purity, piety, and submission. Instead she insisted on reproductive freedom, self-expression, and a voice in public life. In short, the new woman rebelled against patriarchal marriage and, protesting against a social order that was rooted in female biology, she refused to play the role of the ethereal other. Since her demands for personal fulfillment suggested a need for new emotional arrangements, they were seen as threatening the social order. . . .

Brett as New Woman

The new woman's radical challenge to the traditional social structure is seen in Lady Brett Ashley, who has stepped off the pedestal and now roams the world. Entering the public sphere without apology, she dares to frequent places and events previously off limits to her, such as the bar and the bullfight. Gone are the long skirts, bustles,and constricted waists: New clothes designed by Coco Chanel and Erté are intended for movement. The short skirts and light fabrics of the new fashions for women shocked traditionalists. In the spring of 1925, the *New York Times* reported that a woman wearing a dress with transparent sleeves literally caused a riot in London. When she was arrested for indecent exposure and disturbing the peace, the woman protested that such dresses were the fashion in New York City. Similarly, when Brett appears with bare shoulders in Montoya's bar in Pamplona, she deeply offends him; her exposed flesh marks her as a fallen woman.

In spite of the fact that Brett tries to break free of patriarchal control, she often vacillates between the extremes of self-abnegation and self-indulgence, and her relationships with her two former husbands, as well as with Mike Campbell, Robert Cohn, and even Jake, are filled with ambivalence, anxiety, and frequently alienation. Although Brett has the distinction of having married into the British aristocracy, her protected social status has proved to be inversely proportional to her personal satisfaction. As she bitterly observes, "I had such a hell of a happy life with the British aristocracy." As she tries to find her way between the Scylla of social constraint and the Charybdis of chaotic freedom [i.e., choosing between two hazardous alternatives], her search for a new direction is not validated by the social world in which she lives. . . .

Brett's loose, disordered relationships reflects the shattered unity and contradictions of the modern world. On the one hand, she is insouciant, careless, a femme fatale—a woman dangerous to men; on the other, she reflexively lapses into the role of redemptive woman by trying to save men through her sexuality. Mike observes that Brett "loves looking after people," and she has an affair with Robert Cohn because she feels sorry for him and hopes that a romantic interlude will lift his spirits. When he persists in playing the knight who wants to rescue his damsel in distress, she scorns him for his inability to accept episodic or casual sex. In many respects, Brett represents Hemingway's idealized rendering of the woman free of sexual repression. . . .

Challenging Traditional Sexuality

In the 1920s, [Sigmund] Freud's theories of repression were used to justify free love. Contradicting traditional theories of sexuality in the 1920s based on male sexual drive and female receptivity, Brett represents the principle of female eros unbounded by patriarchal control; her closest friend and "true love" is a man who is physically impotent due to a war wound. Many critics have equated Jake's sexual disability with Hemingway's fear of inadequacy, but Jake's affliction has more cultural than biographical significance. His sexual impotence is a sign of loss of masculine power and authority and the axiomatic right to exercise social control. Since Jake's war wound has made it impossible for him to make a physical claim on Brett, he is the only man in the novel who does not try to possess her.

One of the important observations about sexual politics in the novel is that masculine eroticism confines women; therefore, Hemingway implies that sex and friendship are inversely related. In traditional courtship situations, the woman's power is the power to be pursued: once caught, she forfeits her opportunity to choose. Here there are parallels with economic processes: by retaining the interest of multiple suitors, Brett keeps her options open, diversifies her investment of social and sexual energy, and thereby maximizes her opportunities.

Interestingly, Brett breaks up her relationships when her lovers attempt to claim her, that is, to exercise authority over her. She even leaves the bullfighter Romero—a man to whom she is overwhelmingly attracted—when he shows signs of wanting to domesticate her: He tells her to give up her mannish felt hat, to let her hair grow long, to wear more modest clothes. But she has rejected the ideal of female dependence and delicacy: "He wanted me to grow my hair out. Me, with long hair. I'd look so like hell."

Brett prides herself on her daring; for example, she is exceptional in her willingness to take sexual risks. Nevertheless, she is still caught between two modes of gender representation: that of the idealized woman on the pedestal and that of the self-reliant modern woman. She is both the idealized other whom men seek as a prize for their prowess and the autonomous woman who tries to make her own decisions. Although she has broken the connection between moral and physical purity, she still plays the redemptive role of trying to save men through her sexuality—the modern counterpart of Victorian feminine spirituality. In spite of the fact that she is no longer confined to the claustrophobic patriarchal house that in nineteenth-century feminist iconography was the place of entrapment, like the jazz age flapper she has not yet (nor have her male counterparts, for that matter) redefined the traditional relationships of sex and money. Brett has some money from her second husband, from whom she has separated; she also depends on her ability to attract men who will pay for her drinks, her dinners, her taxis and trains. And just as she expects men to pay for many of her pleasures, most of the men in the novel are also bound by the traditional code to assume financial responsibility for women in exchange for their attention. If Brett has gained a measure of freedom in leaving the traditional household, she is still very much dependent on men, who provide an arena in which she can be attractive and socially active as well as financially secure. . . .

In her exchange of sexual and psychological attention with men in return for their financial favors and protection, Brett mirrors both the traditional wife and the prostitute. Yet she will be neither—she will not submit to the authority or the direction of men, nor will she take money in payment for sex because that would be prostitution. In this transition among wife, mistress, and free woman, Brett and the other women in this novel—Frances, Georgette, and Edna—sometimes find themselves in awkward and contradictory roles. Interestingly, radical feminists and prostitutes themselves have argued that marriage is a sanctioned exchange of sex and nurturance for financial protection and social status and that this basic economic transaction is obscured by sentimental ideology, but Brett shields herself from that knowledge. Although she chooses willed ignorance, she does manage to challenge successfully the male control of female eros.

Money as Metaphor

Hemingway gives considerable attention to financial matters in *The Sun Also Rises*; in this novel, money and morality are closely intertwined. Both Jake and the count, who has been in "seven wars and four revolutions" and has arrow wounds to prove it, share the conviction that the confrontation with death has intensified their appreciation of life. By paying the ultimate price—risking death—they have earned the right to appreciate life. As the count remarks:

> "You see, Mr. Barnes, it is because I have lived very much that now I can enjoy everything so well. Don't you find it like that?"

> "Yes, absolutely."

> "I know," said the Count, "That is the secret. You must get to know the values."

Brett, who has less experience, less money, and therefore less control over the circumstances of her life, questions this economic reductionism: "Doesn't anything ever happen to your values?" The count, who is buffered by both his wide experience and his considerable fortune, answers, "No, not any more." His financial and emotional priorities are established, and he has even factored in the cost of falling in love. Aptly titled, the count estimates the cost—psychological as well as economic—of his experiences and consciously decides what price he is willing to pay. So, economic independence and psychological freedom are correlated, and it is the men in this novel who control most of the money. . . .

In contrast to the Scottish aristocrat Mike Campbell, whose entire existence is sustained by debt financing, Jake believes in fiscal and emotional responsibility. Yet he has miscalculated the cost of Brett's lifestyle, and he must ultimately accept the financial and social compromises necessary for her to survive in a rapidly changing world, as well as her effort to forge an individual identity that includes sexual freedom. Jake understands that to be her friend, he must truly relinquish his desire to control her. Because Jake is able to wrestle with this issue of territoriality and possessiveness and to accept his loss of control, he is the only man in the novel who is able to meet Brett on common ground. . . .

Brett and Jake Reverse Roles

In *The Sun Also Rises*, the emotional challenges of Brett and Jake are antithetical: Jake must learn to accept the discomfort and uncertainty that come with his loss of authority, and Brett must learn to make choices for herself and to take responsibility for those choices. In this reworking of traditional psychological patterns, Jake becomes more nurturing and *responsive*, Brett more decisive and *responsible*. This role reversal reflects the changing definitions of gender in the jazz age. In *The Sun Also Rises* men cry and women swear; Brett aggressively expresses her sexual desires, while her lovers wait to be chosen; she likes action—noisy public gatherings, large parties, the blood and gore of the bullfight—whereas the men appreciate the pleasure of sipping brandy in a quiet café.

The loss of traditional cultural meaning is accompanied by a loss of certainty about proper feminine and masculine behavior. Since gender is a social construction, new roles represent a response to new realities, and through trial and error, new forms of sexual behavior emerge. New configurations of gender shatter the old frame, and stripped of their traditional roles, the characters in *The Sun Also Rises* are more transparent, that is, more able to express a greater range of feelings.

Although Hemingway is often stereotyped as a machismo writer, he was fascinated with the variability of the human sexual response and its extraordinary range of expression. . . .

In the context of the new cultural openness—with its new range of ontological possibilities—both Brett and Jake believe in *risk* as the measure of the importance of a choice or action. The true risk taker—the aficionado—is one who is willing to walk the line between life and death in the pursuit of meaning. Yet *afición*—passion—also means certain suffering. For Jake, *afición* is a commitment without reservation to the dangers of the bullfight, and for him, Pedro Romero is the heroic exemplar of masculine courage in his willingness to face the bull without reservation, without protection: "Romero had the old thing, the holdings of his purity of line through the maximum of exposure." But Romero is a *boy*; he is nineteen and not yet fully aware of the meaning or dangers of the risks he takes. He is protected, in part, by his innocence.

Brett's affairs represent the kind of risk taking for her that the confrontation with the bull represents for Romero; by exercising sexual freedom she risks disease, pregnancy, ostracism. Brett's freedom of choice leads to what I would call an anxiety of opportunity, and her response is regressive. Ironically, in spite of her many options, when she does choose for herself, she selects Romero, a traditional man in the person of a nineteen-year-old bullfighter. Although Brett has chosen Romero for deeply personal reasons (she explains to Jake, "I've got to do something I really want to do. I've lost my self-respect"), she recognizes that with this choice comes certain suffering. As she phrases it, "I'm a goner." But this female version of romantic agony is based on the capacity to endure pain. And her final triumph in this scenario of self-denial is to relinquish Romero. . . .

New Models for Male/Female Relationships

Brett's statement at the conclusion of the novel, "we would have had such a damned good time together," and Jake's response, "Isn't it pretty to think so?" have partly biographical, partly historical origins. After concluding *The Sun Also Rises*, Hemingway divorced Hadley in order to marry the very wealthy Pauline Pfeiffer, with whom he went on fishing expeditions and safaris. In sharp contrast to [American author Nathaniel] Hawthorne, who needed the protective sanctity of his home and the gentle ministrations of [his wife] Sophia, Hemingway left his domestic life (and felt *extremely* guilty about doing so) in order to live a more exciting and adventurous existence. The conclusion of *The Sun Also Rises* reflects his conviction that there was no going back for him and, for that matter, no turning back the tide of history for the new woman *and* the new man. Jake and Brett want to want the dream of pastoral simplicity and domestic harmony—but, in fact, they don't.

In spite of the fact that traditional ideals are rejected in this novel, *The Sun Also Rises* concludes with an abatement of tensions between Brett and Jake that is the beginning of genuine friendship. As Jake and Brett toast each other with their "coldly beaded" glasses, they experience the deep mutuality that Bill and Jake share when they drink from the "moisture beaded" wine bottles that had been cooled in the Irati River. Significantly, Brett and Jake do not discover this mutuality in idealized pastoral space; instead, they acknowledge each other as emotional equals while enjoying the civility of the bar in the Palace Hotel in Madrid. This sharing of public space signals the possibility of new kinds of relationships for women and men in the twentieth century.

The Complex Character of Lady Brett Ashley

Nancy R. Comley and Robert Scholes

The authors quote from Ernest Hemingway's mother's letter to him on his twenty-first birthday in which she uses financial metaphors to urge him to get on with his life—to stop "borrowing with no thought of returning." They contend that her early instruction in values influenced Hemingway, who equated financial with emotional qualities in his work. In The Sun Also Rises, *there are characters like Jake Barnes who pay their own way, and there are others who do not. Brett, the authors contend, is a complex character. She is often being bailed out financially, but she is shown to pay emotionally. Hemingway gives her positive and negative characteristics traditionally associated with both sexes. Nancy R. Comley is a professor of English at Queens College of the City University of New York and Robert Scholes is a professor of comparative literature at Brown University.*

If the male figures who populate the Hemingway text [the body of Hemingway's work] emerge from some no-man's-land in the struggle between boyhood and paternity, what is the source of his textual females? The case we shall argue—sometimes explicitly, sometimes implicitly—is that, to a much greater extent than most writers of his stature, Hemingway worked all his life with a relatively simple repertory of male and female figures, modifying and individuating them with minimalist economy. The construction of this limited repertory company began for him with the family and its basic subject positions: father, mother, sister, brother. Hemingway's problem as a writer was to learn how to extend his range to

Nancy R. Comley and Robert Scholes, "Mothers, Nurses, Bitches, Girls, and Devils," *Hemingway's Genders: Rereading the Hemingway Text*, London: Yale University Press, 1994, pp. 23–72. Copyright © 1994 by Yale University. All rights reserved. Reproduced by permission.

figures who were not already given by the family romance. Specifically, it was a problem in the representation of the two figures denied or repressed by familial positioning and the incest taboo: the male and female who may be either the subjects or the objects of sexual desire. . . .

Ernest Hemingway's mother was Grace Hall Hemingway. We can picture young Ernest and his family in church on a Sunday, listening to their Congregationalist minister, the Reverend William E. Barton, proclaiming Christ's compatibility with free enterprise. . . . These matters are important because, within the Hemingway family, it was Grace who took the lead in the attempt to transform the Reverend Barton's capitalist Christianity into a code of conduct.

A Mother's Love Is "Like a Bank"

No one believed more strongly in Barton's Midwestern version of the Protestant ethic than Grace Hall Hemingway. As in so many American families, Mummy was primarily responsible for setting the moral tone while Papa, whose own moral stance was highly conservative, nonetheless performed some version of "lighting out for the territory." In the Hemingway household, Clarence instructed his son about hunting, fishing, and butchering. Grace did the heavy work on the Code. Her values, cast in the rhetoric of the Reverend Barton, pervade the letter she presented to her son, in whom she was not—and with good reason—well pleased, on the occasion of his twenty-first birthday, his nominal entry into manhood. She began by informing him that a mother's love is "like a bank" and that her children are each born "with a large and prosperous Bank Account, seemingly inexhaustible." During a child's first five years he draws continuously on this account as his mother acts almost as "a body slave to his every whim." Then, up to adolescence, the child continues to draw heavily for emotional support and guidance, making only "a few deposits of pennies" in the form of little services and "thank-yous." During the trying time of adolescence, the child turns on her, disregarding her advice, but she bears all this and hopes for the best. Such behavior, however, leaves the bank account "perilously low." Yet now that her child has reached manhood, Grace tells him, the bank is still paying out, a process that cannot continue. . . .

> Unless you, my son Ernest, come to yourself, cease your lazy loafing, and pleasure seeking,—borrowing with no thought of returning;—Stop trying to graft a living off anybody and everybody, spending all your earnings lavishly and wastefully on luxuries for yourself. Stop trading on your handsome face, to fool gullable little girls, and neglecting your duties to God and your Savior Jesus Christ, unless, in other words, you come into your manhood,—there is nothing before you but bankruptcy.

> *You have overdrawn.* . . .

Grace Hemingway is not, in the quoted letter, simply extending the Protestant ethic into a Banking Theory of Mother Love, she is also declaring her son bankrupt. In addition to this, as it happens, she is providing a model of how emotional qualities may be reduced to economic quantities—a formula her son would adapt to his own purposes in fiction and in life. . . .

Brett as Bitch

The action of *The Sun Also Rises* opens with Jake Barnes picking up a Paris prostitute, his companion for the evening. This serves as the outer frame for the introduction of Brett; the inner frame is of bitchy dinner conversation and the actual introduction of Brett as the centerpiece in a garland of gay young men. The framing alerts us to read Brett in terms of both a bitchiness and a sexuality that are different from what might be considered normal for women of her position. Not that she is to be seen as representing bitchiness, prostitution, or homosexuality but that she should be seen in relation to these concepts. Like her gypsy proto-type, Carmen, Brett is "unfeminine" in her usurping of the male prerogative of promiscuity on her own terms. And the question of whether or not she is a bitch is, in her own view and in that of the text in which she is represented, the central ethical issue of her life. Brett first appears in *The Sun Also Rises* entering a dance club while surrounded by homosexual men, a crowd with whom "one can drink in such safety," as she puts it. Jake Barnes has brought his dinner companion, Georgette, a prostitute he will not touch nor allow to touch him: "You sick?" she asks, and when he says he is, she replies, "Everybody's sick. I'm sick, too." Georgette is swept off to the dance floor by the homosexuals, who are happy to dance with her. Jake, who dislikes them, sees them synecdochically, as fragments of men: "I could see their hands and newly washed, wavy hair in the light from the door. . . . As they went in, under the light I saw white hands, wavy hair, white faces, grimacing, gesturing, talking." Disliking their bodies, Jake disembodies them: "Somehow they made me angry. I know they are supposed to be amusing, and you should be tolerant, but I wanted to swing on one, any one, anything to shatter that superior, simpering composure."

Why such anger? Perhaps because the homosexuals are built like "normal" men yet (Jake might think) do not choose to be "normal," while Jake, who has a "normal" male's sex drive, has been left only fragments of sexual apparatus. He cannot perform, though he desires to do so, while the homosexuals can perform and yet do not desire "normal" heterosexual sex. The sexually fragmented Jake is thus linked to men he perceives in fragments as unmanly because he has himself been unmanned. Indeed, his wound has put him in the passive feminine position of lack and has put Brett in the active position of finding men to provide the apparatus that Jake has lost. Although Brett can maintain a kind of objectivity about her sexual engagements, she suffers from being in love with

Runners crowd the street in front of a pack of bulls during the San Fermin festival in Pamplona, Spain. The festival, famed for its daily bullruns and all-night street parties, dates back to the late sixteenth century, but gained world fame from The Sun Also Rises. *AP Images.*

Jake; while he may find being in love "enjoyable," Brett thinks "it's hell on earth." Yet she must see Jake, and however painful that must be for her, she is willing to pay the price for it. In this novel, the insiders are those who pay their own way and who know the values. While Jake is always careful to pay his own way, as the detailing of his financial transactions makes clear, Brett is frequently being bailed out financially. But her lack of ready cash is beside the point, for Brett has paid in other ways and continues to pay emotionally. After a bout of drinking, Jake muses on this aspect of sexual difference: "I thought I had paid for everything. Not like the woman pays and pays and pays. No idea of retribution or punishment."

In the economy of the text Brett goes on paying even while functioning as a highly valued object of desire. The centrality of her position is played out at the height of the fiesta—which is, with its bullfights, an avatar of ancient fertility rites—when Brett is chosen by the garlic-wreathed riau-riau dancers as "an image to dance around." She functions here as an unlikely vestal virgin in these ancient rites, and she succumbs to their power, as exemplified by Pedro Romero, the handsome young bullfighter whom she perceives as the phallus personified. Irresistibly drawn to him, she enlists Jake's aid in this sexual affair. "I don't say it's right. It is right though for me. God knows, I've never felt such a bitch." Romero is drawn to her as well, and he wants to marry her and make her "more womanly" by having her hair grow out. She eventually leaves Romero because she knows that she will be bad for him: "I'm not going to be one of those bitches that ruins children." She has no religion and not much money, but Brett does have a code of ethics; having partially recovered from her affair with Romero, she tells Jake, "You know it makes one feel rather good deciding not to be a bitch. . . . It's sort of what we have instead of God." As her earlier statement indicates, Brett has demythologized Romero from the perfect phallus to the very young man that he is. She thus gives up a lover of physical and moral perfection for men who are less than perfect but more her "sort of thing."

Brett Has Manly Characteristics

In Brett's manner of giving up Romero, Hemingway has allotted her a moment of maternal feeling that mitigates her masculine image as a Carmen who loves and leaves whomever she pleases. At the same time, by presenting her as consciously deciding not to be a bitch, Hemingway moves her away from that version of female excess—bitchiness—toward a more manly resignation. What makes Brett interesting as a character is the way that Hemingway has assigned her qualities from both sides of his gendered repertory of typical figures and situated her somewhere between the extremes of good and bad behavior on both scales.

The Nurturing Nature of Lady Brett Ashley

Lorie Watkins Fulton

Lorie Watkins Fulton refutes critics such as Edmund Wilson and Leslie Fiedler, who have labeled Lady Brett Ashley a "bitch." She cites evidence from the text to indicate that Jake is not a reliable narrator when it comes to Brett. Brett's actions throughout the novel prove that she is nurturing, that she is not for sale, that she is witty, open-minded, and generous of spirit. She is a complex character, fully worthy of Jake's love and friendship. Fulton concludes that the friendship between Brett and Jake could not exist if they were able to have a sexual relationship—Jake would simply become just another of her lovers. Fulton teaches at the University of Mississippi.

Contradiction lies at the heart of *The Sun Also Rises*. This is apparent before the narrative action even begins; Hemingway pairs Gertrude Stein's famed phrase about the "lost" post-war generation ["You are all a lost generation."] with the very different verse from Ecclesiastes emphasizing regeneration ["One generation passeth away, and another generation cometh; but the earth abideth forever. . . ."]. The novel begins with a two-part epigraph at odds with itself. Hemingway's plot also turns on contradictory notions. In this story that he considered a tragedy, everyone celebrates but no one finds true happiness. Through the seemingly pointless pursuit of pleasure, each character searches for meaning in a post-war world that denies the possibility of any sort of meaning at all. Most paradoxically, the novel's protagonist, Jake Barnes, tries to define himself as a man even as a war-related genital wound denies him the most basic assertion of manhood, sexual grati-

Lorie Watkins Fulton, "Reading around Jake's Narration: Brett Ashley and *The Sun Also Rises*," *The Hemingway Review*, vol. 24, fall 2004, pp. 61–80. Copyright © 2004 The Ernest Hemingway Foundation. Reproduced by permission.

fication. Given this depth of contradiction, it seems odd that critics have taken Brett Ashley, the novel's other major character, at face value for so long. Brett is one of Hemingway's richest female characters; her personality gradually emerges as an intriguing mix of femininity and masculinity, strength and vulnerability, morality and dissolution. . . .

Jake Is an Unreliable Narrator

[Misinterpretations] stem from the fact that we as readers see Brett as Jake sees her, and his ideas about Brett seem conflicted at best. . . . But maybe we should question Jake's narration as it pertains to Brett. He seems, perhaps unconsciously, to associate women with manipulation. For example, as he walks "down the Boulevard to the Rue Soufflot" early one morning he notices "flower-women [. . .] arranging their daily stock" and a puppeteer's "girl assistant" as she "manipulate[s]" the vendor's toys. After all, Jake emphatically says more than once, "To hell with Brett. To hell with you, Lady Ashley." His dismissal sounds like an attempt to convince himself of her worthlessness, and this attitude could color his narration, which certainly seems questionable in other respects. In the excised original opening of the novel, Jake even admits that his narration will not "be splendid and cool and detached" because he "made the unfortunate mistake, for a writer, of first having been Mr. Jake Barnes." Jake more subtly points to his own unreliability concerning Brett later when he reflects, "Somehow I feel I have not shown Robert Cohn clearly. The reason is that until he fell in love with Brett, I never heard him make one remark that would, in any way, detach him from other people." Jake tellingly connects his misrepresentation of Cohn to Cohn's falling in love with Brett. If this affair so skewed Jake's perception of Cohn, what must it have done to his feelings about her?

Jake all but admits that he blames his desire for Brett on Brett herself. "Probably I never would have had any trouble if

I hadn't run into Brett when they shipped me to England. I suppose she only wanted what she couldn't have." Besides showing that Jake holds Brett responsible for his unhappiness, his statement points ironically to a seldom-acknowledged equality of purpose between these two characters. In desiring Brett, he too longs for that which he cannot have. A damning example of Jake's biased narration appears in chapter seventeen, detailing events surrounding the fiesta. Just after Brett begins her affair with bullfighter Pedro Romero, Jake sees her "coming through the crowd in the square, walking, her head up, as though the fiesta were being staged in her honor, and she found it pleasant and amusing." However, we discover on the next page that he has totally misrepresented her desire for attention; Brett only wants to talk to Jake, and when he suggests a walk through the crowded upper end of the park, the area filled with "fashionably dressed people," she does not want to go because she does not "want staring at just now." In this scene, Jake clearly ascribes motives and emotions to Brett that the text does not support, and he makes other, similar assumptions about her throughout the novel.

Brett's Words Contradict Her Actions

While Jake obviously narrates through his own prejudices, he remains our primary source of information about Brett. Unfortunately, what she actually says provides little insight into her character because she communicates largely with pat British expressions, and her words frequently contradict her actions. For example, she meets Jake in the bal musette [bar] and says that she plans never "to get tight [drunk] any more" and then orders a brandy and soda with her next breath. Jake obviously knows more about Brett than he directly reveals. When Cohn asserts that Brett would never "marry anybody she didn't love," Jake replies "She's done it twice," giving us a piece of information about her life outside the text. Readers familiar with the excised first chapter know that before she married Lord Ashley, Brett divorced a husband whom she had married "to get away from home," but neither this first husband nor the implication that Brett experienced a problematic childhood appear in the published novel. The extremely daunting problem for readers longing for a glimpse of the "real" Brett Ashley, then, lies in knowing how to extricate valuable information from Jake's narrative prejudices. . . .

Jake's narration frequently seems to "talk around" Brett. By searching for the submerged facets of her character, the unseen portion of that fabled Hemingway iceberg, readers can penetrate Jake's sketchy, prejudiced narration and begin to value Brett as a fully developed character engaged, like Jake, in learning how to live in a world where the rules have irrevocably changed.

Brett Is Nurturing, Not Destructive

By resisting different critical charges against Brett and reexamining the basis for those charges within the text we can begin to uncover concealed aspects of her character. The most damning critical charges against Brett, the ones that delineate her as a "bitch" with devastating powers, seem rooted in two portions of the text: Jake's aforementioned assertion that he would probably have had no problems after his injury had he not met Brett, and Cohn's description of Brett as Circe, the goddess who turns men into swine. These constructions of Brett, however, go against the logic of the text. Obviously, she did not cause Jake's real problem, his wound, and Cohn, who according to Jake "had been thinking for months about leaving his wife and had not done it because it would be too cruel to deprive her of himself," almost certainly became a pig long before he met Brett.

Moreover, Brett's actions prove that she attempts to nurture others, not destroy them. . . . While some feel that Brett mothers those around her in an attempt to provide some sort of sexual healing, her actions certainly satisfy something within herself as well. She frequently chastises Mike and patronizes him almost as she would a small child. When she attempts to placate him after he first confronts Cohn she says, "Don't spoil the fiesta" in much the same way she might say "play nicely" to a toddler. As she leaves the group to nurse Romero after his fight with Cohn, she charges Jake with the task of watching out for Mike, but she still "look[s] in" on Mike herself on at least one other occasion. Furthermore, readers know that Brett nursed Jake through his recovery in a military hospital, and Mike says that his relationship with Brett also began because she "was looking after me."

Brett Is Not Vain

Another critical misconception about Brett assumes that she is vain about her personal appearance. Jake presents her as a primarily self-interested individual who uses her beauty as a weapon and to "add [. . .] up" her conquests. . . . Jake emphasizes the powerful effect of Brett's beauty upon everyone who sees her. When Cohn first meets Brett, he gazes upon her with "eager, deserving expectation" as if he "saw the promised land." He later tells Jake that he finds her "remarkably attractive," and that she possesses a "certain fineness." Count Mippipopolous alludes to a quality similar to that "certain fineness" when he remarks, "You got class all over you." Bill Gorton first says upon seeing Brett, "Beautiful lady," and even the women who work in the wine shop in Pamplona, apparently awed by Brett's appearance, come to the window and stare at her when she first walks down the street. . . .

While the text makes much of Brett's attractiveness, she seems somewhat less sure of her appearance. . . . Brett agrees with Jake's assertion that she likes to "add [. . .] up" her conquests, but possibly because they afford her a much-needed source of reassurance. In the excised text, the omniscient narrator (whom Hemingway only later identifies as Jake) reveals the nontraditional nature of Brett's beauty: "She was not supposed to be beautiful, but in a room with women who were supposed to be beautiful she killed their looks entirely. Men thought she was lovely looking, and women called her striking looking." Perhaps because her attractiveness does not conform to traditional standards of beauty, Brett considers that "her looks were not much" and feels flattered when various artists ask her to sit for them. This deleted information casts a very different light upon how Brett views herself. For example, when Mike asks Jake, "Don't you think she's beautiful?" Brett's response, "Beautiful. With this nose?", no longer seems a ploy to generate further compliments. In fact, her self-deprecating question may conceal a genuine insecurity about her appearance. Another sign of this uncertainty appears in Brett's reluctance to allow the riau-riau dancers to encircle her. She seems uncomfortable when they choose her as "an image to dance around," and instead wants to join the dance herself. Like Romero in the similar scene occurring after he kills the bull that killed Vicente Girones, if Brett functions as a goddess here, she seems a most unwilling deity.

Some critics connect Brett to the decidedly less powerful figure of the prostitute, rather than the goddess. Even revisionist critics seeking to redeem Brett as a character place her in conjunction with Georgette Hobin, the prostitute Jake entertains before Brett comes onto the scene. The two characters do seem to exchange places as Brett goes off with Jake and Georgette remains with Brett's homosexual friends, but there is a distinct difference between the two women—Georgette can be purchased by the highest bidder, but Brett is not for sale. . . . Although several other men try to purchase her favors, she only accepts things from those who do not want to buy her, or, like Jake, know that they cannot. For example, Brett turns down the count's offer of ten thousand dollars in exchange for accompanying him on a trip to Biarritz, and only accepts things from him after making it clear that he cannot purchase her favors. . . .

Brett Has Many Virtues

A final catchall criticism of Brett linked to Jake's sketchy description of her holds that like many women characters in Hemingway's novels, she is a fundamentally weak, narrowly drawn character. . . .

However, with the exception of Jake, all of Hemingway's characters in *The Sun Also Rises*, male and female alike, seem somewhat narrowly drawn. Jake provides a lot more information about Brett than about male characters such as Bill or Montoya. In fact, Jake gives Brett a depth of character rivaling any other in the novel. She easily seems the most racially tolerant member of the group when she accepts the African-American percussionist at Zelli's as "a great friend of mine" and appreciates him as a "Damn good drummer." Her attitude of acceptance contrasts markedly with Jake's rather racist observation that the drummer "was all teeth and lips." In light of the anti-Semitic humor that Hemingway directs at Cohn, attributing such open-mindedness to Brett might seem a bit of a stretch, but she nevertheless displays an appealing generosity of spirit. Additionally, she exhibits a subtle wit as she delicately pokes fun at the count's speech patterns when she asks "Got many antiquities?" Her word choice recalls the count's earlier observation that Brett has "got class all over" her, as does his reply—"I got a houseful." Hemingway highlights another of Brett's virtues, the ability to keep a secret, through a conversation she has with Mike. While Mike claims that "she tells all the stories that reflect discredit on me," the text proves the groundlessness of his accusation. It's Mike, not Brett, who tells the story about his giving away someone else's war medals in a bar. . . .

Brett Is Engaged in a Quest

By acknowledging the shortsightedness of these and other judgments of Brett, we can begin to recognize that she functions as much more than a player in Jake's quest for self-definition: "I did not care what it [the world] was all about. All I wanted to know was how to live in it. Maybe if you found out how to live in it you learned from that what it was all about." Brett also engages in a quest of her own, a similar pursuit that, in many ways, parallels Jake's. His emphasis on Brett's self-destructive behaviors, though, masks this search by making her appear mentally unbalanced. . . . But no character in this novel seems completely stable emotionally or mentally, and Brett hardly appears more psychologically affected than Jake. . . .

Critics have seen Brett's affairs as everything from a fairly innocuous search for reassurance to evidence of nymphomania. While Brett certainly does enter into these affairs for some type of reassurance, the types of men she chooses as lovers suggest that she also uses her sexuality to search vicariously for meaning. Outside of her relationships with Jake and Mike—the long-standing connections that she maintains as part of her fundamental support system—she chooses to carry out her affairs with men who profess to believe in some sort of moral code. Cohn, the first of Brett's temporary lovers, seems a romantic type basically untouched by war. . . . Brett turns to Count Mippipopolous as her next candidate for a partner. However, she quickly cuts short the possibility of a relationship when he says that love "has got a place in my values." Brett challenges him when she replies, "You haven't any values. You're dead, that's all." Because she vests such hope in the power of love, she cannot conceive of love as only one among many values.

Next, Brett enters into a romance with Romero that seems to have the most promise of any affair in the novel. In addition to his tight green trousers, Romero's belief in the code of the bullfight fires Brett's immediate attraction. When the affair first begins, Brett tells Jake, "I feel altogether changed," and Jake notes that she certainly does look "radiant" and "happy." She seems to have found what she has searched for throughout the novel: great sex with a man who might possibly understand her and, more importantly, help her to understand herself. Predictably, though, she ends this affair as well when Romero tries to remake her into the more womanly sort of partner he desires by urging her to grow her hair longer. Brett remains true to herself, the self that Romero wants to change, and tries to cover her pain when she explains the situation to Jake, joking "Me, with long hair. I'd look so like hell." Given her insecurities about her appearance, when she tells Jake "It was rather a knock his being ashamed of me," she almost certainly understates her reaction. Even though Brett says that Romero would have "gotten used" to the way she looked, she does not totally believe it. Hemingway evidences Brett's uncertainty by way of another of her defensive jokes; when she tells Jake that Romero wanted to marry her, she dryly adds, "After I'd gotten more womanly, of course."

Brett tells Jake that she might have prolonged her liaison with Romero if she "hadn't seen it was bad for him." By deciding not to lead Romero on, she takes an important step in defining a system of belief for herself. When she resolves not "to be one of these bitches that ruins children," she moves toward her own definition of morality, a more promising approach than searching for validation through the beliefs of her various lovers. By equating her ability to choose "not to be a bitch" with "sort of what we have instead of God," she sets about defining her own moral code. [Critic] Gerry Brenner speculates that Brett's decision represents a moral watershed and that with it, she "threatens to be his [Jake's] moral equal if not his superior." Whether Brett becomes morally superior to Jake or not, her decision to define her own morality indicates that like him, she definitely searches for a way to make sense of the changed world around her.

In direct contrast to Brett, Jake seems much less willing to ponder the flexibility of moral categories. During one sleepless night he thinks that morality consisted of "things that made you disgusted afterward" and then decides, "No, that must be immorality," before dismissing the topic entirely as "a lot of bilge." The way Jake quickly pushes the issue aside suggests that his search for a fulfilling life will be less successful than Brett's. With her analytical nature, she faces difficulty more readily than Jake does. The odds favor Brett because she can think through and talk out her problems; in contrast, Jake simply avoids thinking of such things. Until Jake can analyze both his needs and the choices that he makes, he will probably continue to search unsuccessfully for a mode of living that satisfies him.

The Bond Between Jake and Brett

Besides engaging in a quest for self-definition that equals Jake's in significance, Brett also plays a substantial, active role in their relationship. However, because Hemingway depicts the relationship exclusively from Jake's perspective, Brett's role does not become immediately apparent. Jake reveals the depth of his feeling for Brett when his stoic narrative breaks down and he admits that he "was blind, unforgivingly jealous of what had happened to" Cohn. But what, exactly, does Jake envy? Jake does not begrudge Cohn the sex alone, or he would hate Mike equally; Jake must resent Cohn because he can both love Brett and have sex with her, something Jake knows he can never do. Because readers know how Jake feels about Brett, and that his love for her results in many a sleepless night, he easily garners our sympathy. As a result, Brett sometimes comes off as a tease, leading Jake on and using him for entertainment when she does not have a lover.

Approaching the relationship from a more objective perspective, however, broadens the possibilities. If readers can get past the emotional bias of Jake's narration, the bond between him and Brett seems much more symbiotic than his description indicates. Hemingway suggests that a value exists in the relationship which Jake cannot see because of his own impossible desire. Readers know that Brett values Jake highly. While her lovers come and go, her relationship with Jake remains constant. When she tries to stay away from him, she cannot, and Brett even says that she does not see Jake because she wants to, but because she has to. Hemingway demonstrates her dependence on Jake when, in a fruitless attempt to separate from him, she leaves for San Sebastian with Cohn. The night before she leaves, she tells Jake that she must go because their parting will create a more positive situation, "Better for you. Better for me." When she returns, she acknowledges the futility of her attempt by looking directly at Jake and saying, "I was a fool to go away." ... Jake's stance of ironic detachment is his most effective tool for masking his own dependence. Readers can observe this attitude clearly in thoughts like the one he has after receiving Brett's telegram near the novel's end: "That was it. Send a girl off with one man. Introduce her to another to go off with him. Now go and bring her back. And sign the wire with love. That was it all right."

While Jake's stoic attitude successfully distances him, readers can still discern the depths of his desire when he occasionally drops his detached pose. Hemingway depicts one such instance after Brett leaves with Romero and Jake observes, "The three of us [Jake, Bill, and Mike] sat at the table, and it seemed as though about six people were missing." Jake's actions after the fiesta further betray his need for Brett. He implies that he lingers in nearby San Sebastian because he suspects that Brett will need him when her affair with Romero reaches its inevitable end, as Jake notes, "I had expected something of the sort." ...

Ironically, however, most of the benefits that Jake derives from their association involve sex. Most obviously, Brett provides Jake with a convenient way to maintain a pretense of social normalcy concerning his sexuality. While Jake's friends know about his injury, Brett provides a useful cover for him with various acquaintances, like the count, that do not. For instance, when the count asks why Jake and Brett do not marry, she deflects his question with the rather inane excuse, "We have our careers." . . .

The main advantage Jake derives from his connection to Brett, however, seems as much psychological as sexual; she gives him a legitimate focus for mourning what has happened to him. Hemingway demonstrates this early in the novel as Jake lies in bed thinking of his injury:

> I lay awake thinking and my mind jumping around. Then I couldn't keep away from it, and I started to think about Brett and all the rest of it went away. I was thinking about Brett and my mind stopped jumping around and started to go in sort of smooth waves. Then all of a sudden I started to cry.

Contemplating Brett allows the stoic Jake to feel the pain of all that he has lost in a way he can accept. He repeatedly dismisses any reference to his injury with a joke, but thinking of Brett allows him to refocus the pain caused by his "shameful" wound. Wanting the woman he cannot have appears infinitely more acceptable to him than grieving the sexuality he has lost. More importantly, with Brett, Jake can commiserate with someone who truly loves him and mourns his loss almost as much as he does.

Brett must possess truly extraordinary qualities to occupy such a prominent position in Jake's life; however, she also represents all that he can never have, and she sometimes appears as a "bitch" or "narrowly drawn" character because his conflicted mind projects that image of her. If we read beyond Jake's narrative bias we can see that Hemingway creates Brett as a character worthy of Jake's devotion, a real woman with complexities equaling his own. . . .

Friendship Trumps Sexual Love

Jake cannot make love to Brett, but in spite of that, or perhaps because of it, he becomes the only man she actually talks to. When Brett tells Jake, just before she begins her affair with Romero, "You're the only person I've got, and I feel rather awful to-night," she acknowledges that only Jake understands her, or even tries to.

Clearly, Hemingway has already put the fundamentals of a friendship into place; Brett and Jake have shared the tragic experience of war, and, as a result, they listen to and support one another in their own ways. Friendship ultimately presents the only option for them; when Jake proposes a more serious commitment, that they "just live together," Brett refuses, remarking, "I don't think so. I'd just tromper you [be unfaithful to you] with everybody. You couldn't stand it." She values her connection with Jake too much to jeopardize it with such an experiment, and even Jake acknowledges the proximity of friendship to love when he thinks, "you had to be in love with a woman to have a basis of friendship." In fact, he might even unconsciously rank friendship as superior to love; his equation sets love as the basis of friendship, and thus establishes friendship as the more advanced, developed relationship.

Read through the lens of this friendship, the novel's concluding scene seems more optimistic than readers commonly think. . . . Hemingway implies that the real tragedy is the likelihood that if Jake possessed full sexual capabilities, his deep connection to Brett could not exist. Brett seems unaware of this probability when she laments that she and Jake "could have had such a damned good time together." Conversely, Jake's oft-quoted response, "Isn't it pretty to think so?," suggests his belief that the romantic relationship could never have flourished long-term. While it might seem pleasant to think that this narrative could have ended happily if only Jake had escaped the war unscathed, he has already eliminated this possibility. Brett earlier says that Jake "wouldn't behave badly" if she rejected him; in response, Jake replies without hesitation, "I'd be as big an ass as Cohn." In the end, Hemingway intimates that if Jake could have a sexual relationship with Brett, then he would become just another of her lovers, a passing distraction doomed to an eventual rejection. Given this likelihood, if readers view the couple's relationship as an unrealized friendship, it becomes something to celebrate rather than lament. By transcending the physical, their connection represents the possibility for a true, lasting camaraderie, a stable connection offering each of them something much more substantial than the sexual union that they think they desire. Freed from the limits of Jake's perspective, we as readers can see that Hemingway has bound these two characters together for life. Their friendship will help them to survive, and indeed has already contributed to their healing. This mutually beneficial connection becomes more significant and lasting than any romantic relationship in the novel. As such, it might form part of Brett's alternative, post-war morality, part of "what we have instead of God."

Blended Gender Roles in
The Sun Also Rises

Sibbie O'Sullivan

The author, a poet and senior lecturer at the University of Mary-land, argues that rather than being a novel about the death of love, The Sun Also Rises *is a book about the survival of love and friendship. She traces two kinds of love and friendship in the book: the heterosexual relationship of Brett and Jake and the male-male friendships Jake shares with Bill Gorton and Wilson-Harris. Sibbie O'Sullivan points out that parallels exist between heterosexual love and male bonding. Although imperfect, Brett and Jake's relationship has been tested and is lasting. In O'Sullivan's view, their relationship, along with the bullfights, are the only things of permanence in the book.*

It would be naive to say that *The Sun Also Rises* is a joyous book, or even a hopeful one; it is, of course, neither. Most often interpreted as a picture of post-war aimlessness and anomie, Hemingway's 1926 novel is usually said to be the bible of the Lost Generation, a modern-day courtesy book on how to behave in the waste land Europe had become after the Great War. However valid this interpretation may be, it is limiting and unduly pessimistic. It necessitates a particularly negative reading of the characters in the book and undervalues Hemingway's intuitive awareness of cultural and historical forces and the impact they have on personal relationships. Most damaging of all, the consensual interpretation fosters the harmful propagation of sexist stereotypes and ignores Hemingway's knowledge of and respect for the New Woman.

Sibbie O'Sullivan, "Love and Friendship/Man and Woman in *The Sun Also Rises*," *Arizona Quarterly*, summer 1988, pp. 76–97. Reprinted in *Ernest Hemingway: Seven Decades of Criticism*, edited by Linda Wagner-Martin, East Lansing, MI: Michigan State University Press, 1998, pp. 61–79. Copyright © 1988 by the Regents of the University of Arizona. Reproduced by permission of the publisher and the author.

Instead of reading *The Sun Also Rises* as the death of love, we can read it as a story about the cautious belief in the survival of the two most basic components of any human relationship: love and friendship. Examined this way, the novel is a rather extraordinary document that unites the two separate sexual spheres of the nineteenth century and in so doing breaks away from the moral imperatives of the Victorian age while demonstrating the possibility of love's survival in the more realistic but nihilist twentieth century.

The coaxial themes of love and friendship inform this book in such subtle ways that they are easily overlooked even though they are the forces which motivate the characters' behavior. In the case of Jake Barnes and Lady Brett Ashley they form the basis of their relationship. Too often this relationship is laid waste by stereotypical thinking. The cliché runs like this: Jake, unmanned in the war, is not only physically but spiritually impotent and allows himself to be debased by Brett, that "non-woman," that "purely destructive force." Such critical abuse is understandable when we realize that Brett is considered part of that long American tradition of the dark-haired, bad woman. She must be termed "promiscuous" and a "nymphomaniac" if her sexual behavior is to be explained at all. The mainspring of such a tradition is that "nice girls don't do it." But we've already seen in the short stories that Hemingway refuses to bind his female characters to such strictures. His women do "do it," and with relish.

Hemingway seems to take for granted that Brett is a sexually active woman. And though he did not consciously set out to create the New Woman, Hemingway's Brett is a fine example of one. . . .

Victorian Male-Female Relationships

The Sun Also Rises reflects the changing sex role patterns prevalent in Western society during the thirty years before its publication. In many ways this first novel is Hemingway's goodbye kiss to the Victorian ethos under which he was raised. . . .

Cohn, of course, is a bridge figure. He lives in the waste land but does not adhere to its values. He represents the dual concepts of manly adventure and romantic love so important in the nineteenth century. When we meet him he is engaged to Frances Clyne, a woman with "the absolute determination that he [Cohn] should marry her." . . .

By focusing the first two chapters on Cohn and the dual concerns of romantic love and adventure, Hemingway establishes a backdrop against which the rest of the book is played. That backdrop becomes, as Cohn's daydream of South America fades, the conventional theme of courtship and marriage—in other words, the typical theme of the Victorian novel. Of course, conventional marriage does little to erode the rigid boundaries between men and women, and Robert and Frances act out scenes which accentuate, in a progressively negative manner, the worst attributes of both sexes. She becomes a nasty woman tremendously afraid of not being married, and he becomes a chump willing to take her verbal abuse lest he break into tears, as he habitually does whenever they "have a scene." The demise of this relationship is nothing less than a wicked parody of the engagement/marriage ritual itself. Fifty pages into the novel we see already that the old way offers nothing but anger and humiliation.

In Chapter II another Victorian ritual is enacted, but with a twist: Jake gets a prostitute but does not sexually use her. As he explains, "I had picked her up because of a vague sentimental idea that it would be nice to eat with some one." Jake's motive is not sexual fulfillment or an escape from a dull marriage bed, but companionship. Prostitute or not, Georgette is recognized by Jake as a fellow human being, not as a mere commodity to buy and discard. But however kindly Jake treats Georgette his actions still reflect the rigid gender roles of the nineteenth century. The underbelly of the conventional Victorian marriage was, after all, prostitution; the erotic restrictions placed on wives encouraged husbands to use whores for sexual release, experimentation, and erotic delight. Coming as it does after the parody of Victorian marriage that Robert Cohn and Frances Clyne represent, this chapter enacts the inevitable decline of such a relationship were it to go on. When Jake introduces Georgette to some acquaintances as his "fiancée" the connection between marriage and prostitution becomes unmistakable.

A New Model for Male-Female Relationships

So far the male-female relationships fall within the scope of the typical Victorian ethos of courtship/marriage, and customer/prostitute. With the entrance of Lady Brett Ashley the focus shifts. Brett's arrival in Chapter III trumpets a new set of relationships. Since Brett is neither a wife nor a prostitute, it is fitting that she emerge from an environment alien to these two opposites; hence she arrives with a group of homosexual men. Her mannishness is thus established through this group, but since she quickly leaves that group and bonds with Jake we learn that her inclinations are orthodox and acceptable. We know that she is not a lesbian, and that her association with male homosexuals, instead of being a detriment, enhances her attractiveness.

As soon as Brett and Jake begin talking we realize theirs is no conventional relationship. Their dialogue bristles with familiarity. Jake asks, "Why aren't you tight? [drunk]" and Brett answers by ordering a drink. The jabs continue:

"It's a fine crowd you're with Brett," I said.

"Aren't they lovely? And you, my dear. Where did you get it?"

The "it," of course, refers to Georgette. As this exchange indicates, Brett and Jake share a public language (remember that

Cohn is with them) that includes mild insult and sarcasm. It is a language in which the indefinite pronouns need not be identified. The verbal volley continues on the dance floor and in the taxi, where, alone at last, Brett confesses to Jake, "Oh, darling, I've been so miserable."

What we know so far about Brett's and Jake's relationship is this. First, as the dialogue reveals, Jake and Brett are friends. No matter what else their relationship may be it has a solid base in friendship; such benign verbal ribbing only takes place between friends. Secondly, they share a history. Reference to Brett's drinking habits and how out of character it is for Jake to pick up a whore indicate a more than superficial knowledge of each other's habits. Thirdly, Brett has control. She neatly declines two dances with Cohn and instigates her and Jake's departure. And fourthly, there seem to be two languages operating for them: public and private. It is by the latter that the truth is revealed.

And the truth isn't pretty. They are in love with each other but because of Jake's wound that love cannot be sexually fulfilled. They have tried making love but failed: "I don't want to go through that hell again." Love is "hell on earth," but they continue to see each other. There is a sense of things being out of control; at the end of the taxi ride Brett is shaky, and later when Jake returns alone to his apartment he cries himself to sleep. When Jake leaves Brett it is at another bar and in the company of another man.

This pattern of public/private behavior shapes Brett's and Jake's relationship in an important way. Jake accepts Brett's need for public display, her need to breeze around Paris with as many men as possible. He also accepts her need to tell him about it privately. After she interrupts his sleep to recap her night's adventure with the Count, Jake, comments to himself, "This was Brett, that I had felt like crying about." Though there is probably disgust in his voice at this point, there is also resignation, resignation that the woman he loves acts in such peculiar and unstable ways.

A parade of World War I veterans moves through Paris, circa 1920. The Sun Also Rises *is set during this post-war era, and its characters, who live in Paris, are part of the "Lost Generation," men and women whose experiences during the war caused them to become psychologically and morally lost.* Henry Guttman/Hulton Archive/Getty Images.

The ability to listen, the capacity to care, are not faculties belonging to Jake alone. Brett is also tender and solicitous in private moments. During her second visit to Jake with Count Mippipopolous, when she sees that Jake is a bit shaky, she sends the Count off to get champagne. As Jake lies face down on the bed Brett gently strokes his head. "Poor old darling. . . . Do you feel better, darling? . . . Lie quiet." Though her actions are kind and genuine, Brett does not allow this moment to blunt the truth. When Jake, perhaps succumbing to her touch, to her motherly devotion, asks, "Couldn't we live together, Brett? Couldn't we just live together?" she answers the only way she knows how:

> "I don't think so. I'd just *tromper* you with everybody. You couldn't stand it."

> "I stand it now."

> "That would be different. It's my fault, Jake. It's the way I'm made."

When the count returns with the champagne all three go out and Jake and Brett talk once more in their public manner until out on the dance floor. Brett, in the privacy of Jake's arms, recites again what is fast becoming her litany, thus closing Book I: "Oh, darling, . . . I'm so miserable."

Merging Gender Roles

These two small scenes are interesting for what they tell us about how easily Brett and Jake merge the traditional sex roles. The two qualities of granting freedom and lending an ear that Jake exhibits in the first scene clash with the stereotypical image of the muscle-bound, closed-mouth husband/boyfriend who "doesn't want to hear about it." If Jake's attentiveness and meekness in the face of Brett's gallivanting seem in some ways feminine (Jake as the suffering wife?), then in the second scene Brett reenacts a particularly masculine ritual, characterized by the "line": "I love you babe, but I can't stay tied to one woman. I'm just that kind of man." Brett's version of this "line," is not delivered with any hint of bravado or cruelty as it has been delivered by men to countless women in books and movies, but as an assessment of, almost as an apology for her personality. What is striking about these role reversals is how easily and naturally they appear and reappear throughout the couple's interactions. Brett's behavior, especially, flows back and forth between being soft and caring, and hard and straight-forward. Jake has the ability to snap back after a painful relapse. Such flexibility is unthinkable in traditional relationships where sex roles are rigid. Robert Cohn and Frances Clyne do not have this kind of flexibility. One reason Brett leaves Romero at the end of the novel is that he demands that she conform to the rigid traditional female role. . . .

There is no reason why Brett's and Jake's behavior should be gauged by traditional gender roles since those roles have been modified to suit the couple's needs. Brett is, after all, the New Woman, and her claim to sexual freedom . . . is both attractive and perplexing to her fellow characters, Jake cannot be the traditional man because he is impotent. Freed from the pressure to prove his worth through sexual intercourse, Jake must develop other means of asserting his personality.

Both Brett and Jake expect little of each other and have a relationship in which they agree to accept each other as they are. Early in the book Jake describes Brett's two worst habits to Robert Cohn: "She's a drunk," and "She's done it twice," (referring to Brett's marrying men "she didn't love.") Brett gives a clear self-assessment when she speaks of her intention to return to Mike: "He's so damned nice and he's so awful. He's my sort of thing." Because Jake accepts Brett as she is he has been able to maintain their relationship for as long as he has. We should remember that Cohn and Pedro Romero do not accept Brett as she is and therefore lose her. Brett, too, accepts Jake as he is. They can never be completely, physically united, and for a woman as sexually alive as Brett this loss is deep and sad.

At the end of Book I the boundaries have been drawn. Brett and Jake, the New Woman and the shattered veteran, conduct a relationship based on the honest assessment of each other's failings. In any other arms Brett's lament of "darling, I'm so miserable" could pass for a comment on the progress of a particular night's activities, but in Jake's arms it is properly received for what it is: a statement about Brett's soul. This kind of emotional shorthand conveyed in private moments through a private language is the backbone of Jake's and Brett's relationship and a testament to its strength. Though imperfect, their friendship is imbued with the survival mechanisms of honesty, shared histories, and serious love.

Male-Male Friendships Bring Quiet Joy

Book II begins by depicting male-male friendships, first in Paris and then in Spain. In many aspects Jake's friendship with Bill Gorton is similar to his with Brett. Though they are frequently separated, the two men can quickly restore intimacy. . . .

Other examples of intense male interaction are the scenes with Wilson-Harris, the English angler Bill and Jake meet in Burguete, and with the aficionados in Pamplona. Wilson-Harris is very candid about how much he likes Bill and Jake. The sheer joy of buying his friends drinks almost overcomes him. At one point he says, "I say Barnes. You don't know what this all means to me." When Jake and Bill leave to return to Pamplona, Wilson-Harris gives them each a present, a valentine of hand-tied fishing flies. . . .

[Noted Hemingway critic and biographer] Carlos Baker and others often divide the novel's characters into two groups: those who are solid, and those who are neurotic. Baker puts Jake, Bill, and Romero in the former category, and Cohn, Brett, and Mike in the latter. As fair as this division may seem to surface, it belies the truth of human interaction and negates the web of friendship in which all characters, at one time or another, are enmeshed. And what a complicated web it is. Throughout the fiesta the characters form new pairs or groups as they partake of the festivities. Everyone at one time or another shares the other's company. Of all the characters Brett seems most in control of choosing her companions. She manuevers it so that, with one exception, she is never alone with Cohn. In contrast, she frequently asks Jake to go off with her alone, by now a rather predictable action. . . .

The separation of the group into two factions creates barriers if not as visible, surely at least, as damaging as those erected between the sexes. Such barriers highlight how friends betray but not how to forgive one another. And in Brett's case, because she is grouped with the neurotics, she suffers under a double onus: she becomes the neurotic female, the "bitch," the "nymphomaniac." Clearly, it is the double standard and nothing else that permits the critics, both male and female, to criticize Brett for sleeping with Cohn and Romero while not criticizing Cohn and Romero for the same act. But Hemingway is not interested in erecting barriers but in destroying them. He does not see behavior as either male or female. Nor does he see passion as something solely inter-sexual. In *The Sun Also Rises*, bonding and passion occur in mysterious ways. There is no difference in the intensity of what Wilson-Harris feels for Jake and Bill and what Brett feels for Romero. Brett, however, is allowed the sexual expression of her intensity whereas Wilson-Harris would not be, even if his feelings were sexual. The bond that Jake establishes with Montoya is special because it is validated both by intensity and physical touch. Though this touch is not overtly sexual it certainly suggests sexuality because it is the symbol of a shared passion, just as the touching of sexual partners represents mutual passion.

The above relationships, considering their brevity, their passion, and the intensity of mutual attraction between their participants, would be like one-night stands or casual affairs, were they to exist in the sexual dimension. I am not suggesting that we belittle the effects of sexual union, or that Brett's escapade with Romero is as inconsequential as Wilson-Harris's fishing trip. What I am suggesting is that there are parallels between male bonding and heterosexual bonding which should not be overlooked, and that both forms of bonding are as easily established as they are destroyed. By removing the sexual barriers which unduly place the burden of bad behavior on sexually active women (as Jake points out the woman pays and pays and pays), we see that Brett's transgression is no worse than Jake's; in fact, Brett's may have fewer repercussions. We can assume with good reason that Mike will take Brett back after her fling with Romero, but we are not as certain about a reconciliation between Jake and Montoya. True to form, Hemingway remains aloof in making clear any moral certainties. But one thing for certain is that Hemingway wants us to look at all the characters' behavior and not just Brett's. The structural parallels in the novel are too clear to ignore.

Openness and Receptivity Are Key to Survival

What seems to be more important than who does what to whom and why is the acceptance of the mysteries of behavior, and of bonding in particular. Those characters who survive the best are the ones who have cultivated a certain sense of negative capability. The ability to accept simultaneously two opposing ideas or modes of behavior becomes a means of survival. Those characters who do not have this capability end up exiled from the web of relationships established at Pamplona. Hence it is Cohn and Romero, those representatives of the traditional male role, who are ultimately excluded from any relationship with Brett, the object of their desires. Rigidity of values and, since these two men were Brett's lovers a corresponding rigidity of erectile tissue, are not what keeps Brett. Jake, it seems, wins again.

Book III opens with Jake's observation that "it was all over." Ostensibly referring to the fiesta, Jake's statement is also an assessment of the condition of the web of relationships woven in the previous two hundred pages. It is in shreds. Brett has taken off with Romero. Cohn has left in disgrace,

Jake is blind drunk for the first time in the novel, and Mike, as we presently discover, is penniless. Book III is, initially, a book of departures, but by the close of the book Jake and Brett have reunited, thus reconstructing the web. . . .

The Cynical Nature of Friendship

Hemingway has said that the more applicable epigraph for his novel is the one from Ecclesiastes ["One generation passeth away and another generation cometh; but the earth abideth forever. . . ."] and not the one attributed to Gertrude Stein ["You are all a lost generation"]. We must take the author's on some things; the very title bears this out. If this novel exhibits traits of Stein's lost generation, it also exhibits the cyclical nature of friendship, its rhythm of disintegration and renewal. Brett's and Jake's relationship may have been dealt a cruel blow by fate or the First World War, but it is anything but lost, sadistic, and sick. It, and the bullfights, are the only lasting things in the book. Contrary to what many readers believe, Brett Ashley is a positive force, a determined yet vulnerable woman who makes an attempt to live honestly. Her struggle in choosing to marry one man while loving another strangely coincides with Hemingway's own dilemma. For a year before the novel's publication he wrestled with whether or not to divorce Hadley Richardson, his first wife, and marry Pauline Pfeiffer.

Hemingway broke with convention by creating a brilliant example of the New Woman and dismantled nineteenth-century gender lines by uniting love with friendship. His masculine ego did not suffer one iota in the process. He, unlike many of his critics, believes as Jake Barnes does: "In the first place, you had to be in love with a woman to have a basis of friendship."

Hemingway Challenges Sexual and Cultural Codes

Debra A. Moddelmog

Debra A. Moddelmog argues that while society and critics frequently try to put gender and sexuality into rigid categories, Ernest Hemingway, both in his life and art, departed from traditional codes of masculinity and femininity, homosexuality and heterosexuality. She offers an interpretation of several key passages from The Sun Also Rises *that connect Brett to lesbianism and Jake to homosexuality. She argues that Hemingway is "putting gender and sexuality into constant motion" despite the efforts of society to define them. Moddelmog is associate professor of English at Ohio State University and the author of numerous works of literary criticism on twentieth-century American writers, including* Reading Desire: In Pursuit of Ernest Hemingway.

Hemingway's life and especially his fiction constantly call into question the validity of society's prescriptions for gender identification and sexual orientation. Ironically, in mapping out this territory of interrogation, I will have to draw upon the very concepts that I claim [*The Sun Also Rises*] problematizes (masculinity/femininity, homosexuality/heterosexuality). . . . But by illustrating how Hemingway's text brings traditional significations of gender and sexuality into conflict, I hope to show that Hemingway's fiction and, ultimately, his life reveal the intellectual limitations that result when "gender" and "sexuality" are read as innocent acts of nature and as fixed binaries.

Debra A. Moddelmog, "Reconstructing Hemingway's Identity: Sexual Politics, the Author, and the Multicultural Classroom," *Narrative*, vol. 1, no. 3, October 1993, pp. 187–206.

Gender and Sexuality in *The Sun Also Rises*

To elucidate this thesis, let us look at an early scene in *The Sun Also Rises* that seems to establish the gender and sexual ideologies upon which the novel will turn: the occasion of Jake and Brett meeting at the dancing club, Jake accompanied by a prostitute, Georgette Hobin, and Brett by a group of homosexual men. In a poststructuralist reading that provides the starting point for mine, Cathy and Arnold Davidson observe that, by switching dancing partners, these characters arrange themselves in different pairings: Jake and Georgette, Jake and Brett, the young men and Brett, the young men and Georgette. These partner exchanges initially suggest "the fundamental equivalence" of the women as well as of the men: Georgette and Brett are conjoined under the pairing of prostitution/promiscuity just as Jake and the young men are connected under the pairing of sexually maimed/homosexual. Consequently, this episode reveals the contradictions in Jake's own life. Jake relies upon the homosexuality of the young men to define his manhood (at least his desire is in the right place), but that definition is tested by the joint presence of Georgette and Brett. As the Davidsons conclude, "The terrifying ambiguity of [Jake's] own sexual limitations and gender preferences may well be one source of his anger (it usually is) with Brett's companions, and another reason why he articulates his anger and hatred for them before he reveals his love for her."

But this perceptive reading illuminates only one of the "fundamental equivalences" set up in this scene; further, it fails to recognize that, as these equivalences multiply, the glue connecting the descriptive pairs loosens. In other words, through a series of interchanges, Jake and Brett are aligned with several equations; the units dissolve as they rearrange themselves into new pairs. What began as an inseparable unit (sexually maimed/homosexual) ends as free-floating signifiers (sexually maimed, homosexual), and the characters, particularly Jake and Brett, are revealed as bodies of contradictions. Ultimately these pairings challenge the validity of gender and sexuality binarisms: masculine/feminine, heterosexual/homosexual.

Brett and Gender-Bending

For instance, the pairing of Brett and Georgette, like the pairing of Jake and the homosexual men, is complex and multifaceted. The resemblance between the two women is underscored when Jake, half-asleep, thinks that Brett, who has come to visit him, is Georgette. Obviously such a correspondence reveals that both women sleep around, one because she believes it is the way she is made, the other because it is the way she makes a living. Yet this explanation of motives reminds us that women's outlets for their desires were closely intertwined with economic necessity in the years following World War I, even in the liberated Left Bank of Paris. As a white, heterosexual, upper-class woman, Brett still must depend, both financially and socially, on hooking up with some man or another. . . .

Brett's self-destructive drinking and her attempts to distance herself from sexual role stereotyping—for example, her short hair is "brushed back like a boy's" and she wears a "man's felt hat"—indicate her resentment of this prescribed arrangement. [Critic] Susan Gubar reminds us that many women artists of the modernist period escaped the strictures of societally defined femininity by appropriating male clothing, which they identified with freedom. For such women, cross-dressing became "a way of ad-dressing and re-dressing the inequities of cultural-defined categories of masculinity and femininity." Brett Ashley fits within this category of women who were crossing gender lines by cross-dressing and behaving in "masculine ways." Indeed, although Brett's wool jersey sweater reveals her to be a woman, the exposure is not enough to counteract the effect of her masculine apparel and appearance on the men around her. Pedro Romero's desire to make her look more "womanly" and to marry him might be explained as the response of a man raised in a culture that requires clear distinctions between the gender roles of men and women. But Mike Campbell's similar attempt to convince Brett to buy a new hat and to marry him suggests that Brett is dangerously close to overturning the categories upon which male and female identity, and patriarchal power, depend. The "new woman" must not venture too far outside old boundaries.

Brett's cross-dressing conveys more than just a social statement about gender. It also evokes suggestions of the transvestism practiced by and associated with lesbians of the time (and since). Although sexologists such as Havelock Ellis, whose works Hemingway was recommending enthusiastically during the 1920s, recognized the Mannish Lesbian as only one kind of lesbian, wearing men's clothing was often viewed as sexual coding—and many lesbians chose to cross-dress in order to announce their sexual preference. Significantly, the parallel to Georgette reinforces Brett's connection to lesbianism. When Jake introduces Georgette to a group seated in the restaurant, he identifies her as his fiancée, Georgette Leblanc. As scholars have noted, Georgette Leblanc was a contemporary singer and actress in Paris—and an acknowledged lesbian. This association consequently deepens the symbolic relationship of Brett to Georgette, linking them in a new equation: independence/lesbian. Brett's transvestism crosses over from gender inversion to sexual sign: Brett desires the lesbian's economic, social, and sexual autonomy.

In fact, Brett's inability to sustain a relationship and her congruent alcoholism might be indications not of nymphomania, with which critics have often charged her, but of a dissatisfaction with the strictures of the male-female relationship. Brett's announcement, for example, that she can drink safely among homosexual men can be taken to mean that she cannot control her own heterosexual desire, but it could also reveal an underlying anxiety toward the heterosexual desire of men. Such an anxiety might be related to her abusive marriage, but that experience need not be its only source. As Brett tells Jake after the break-up with Pedro Romero, "I can't even marry Mike." Of course, soon after she says this, she declares, "I'm going back to Mike. . . . He's so damned nice and he's so awful. He's my sort of thing." Yet even in giving her reasons for returning to Mike, Brett reveals her inner turmoil and ambivalence. Like Mike, she is "nice" and "awful," and the book ends before this promised reunion takes place.

Brett's anxiety about male heterosexual desire should not be conflated with lesbian desire since, typically, the two emotions are not related causally. Brett's lesbianism manifests itself in other ways, however, most immediately through her association with her homosexual companions; as Jake states three times, she is "with them," she is "very much with them." This homosexual identification helps to explain Brett's attraction to Jake who, according to Hemingway in a letter written in 1951, has lost his penis, but not his testicles and spermatic cord—and thus not his sexual desire. If we accept this explanation, Jake lacks the feature that has traditionally been the most important in distinguishing sex as well as male sexual desire. He is a sexual invalid and, as a consequence, sexually in-valid. Jake's sex, gender, and sexuality, conflated as one under the law of compulsory heterosexuality, are thereby separated and problematized. Like a woman, Jake has no penis to thrust into Brett. Instead, Brett ministers to him, rubbing his head as he lies on the bed, and recognizes that the absent male sex organ makes Jake different from other suitors. In this context, Jake's notion that Brett "only wanted what she couldn't have" takes on added meaning. Besides non-penile sex, she wants to find some way to accommodate the fluidity of sex and gender that characterizes her desire and her condition.

Brett's affiliation with the homosexual men and her gender-bending complicate, in turn, Jake's relationship with her. Jake calls Brett "damned good-looking" and describes her hair as being "brushed back like a boy's," two attributions that dissolve into one in Jake's later identification of Pedro Romero as "a damned good-looking boy." Jake's desire for Brett can thus be partially explained as homosexual, a desire that seems about to break through the surface of Jake's narrative at any time. . . .

Jake and Homosexuality

Jake's relationships with Bill Gorton and Pedro Romero constitute two of the more important sources of sublimated homosexuality. During their fishing trip to the Irati River, Bill tells Jake. "Listen. You're a hell of a good guy, and I'm fonder of you than anybody on earth. I couldn't tell you that in New York. It'd mean I was a faggot." In expressing his fondness for Jake, Bill realizes the risk he takes in declaring his strong feelings for another man: his words might be construed as an admission of homosexual love. To avoid being interpreted in that way, Bill must declare homosexual desire an impossibility. However, Bill's phrasing in this passage and his subsequent focus on homosexuality suggest that such desire is a possibility. For one, his statement "I'm fonder of you than anybody on earth" can be read as "I'm fonder of you than I am of anybody else on earth" or as "I'm fonder of you than anybody else is." Either reading elevates Bill and Jake's relationship to a primary position; it is a connection more binding and important than any other relationship Bill has formed.

In addition, Bill's view that disclosing his affection for Jake would, in New York, mean that he is "a faggot" indicates Bill's awareness of the permeability of the line separating homosocial and homosexual behavior and desire. Outside the geographic and psychological boundaries of America and its strict morality. Bill's feelings are platonic; inside those boundaries, they are homosexual. Bill's confusion about the boundaries for same-sex relationships suggests that he cannot be sure about the "purity" of his feelings for Jake or of Jake's for him. Having stated his fondness. Bill immediately moves the discussion away from their relationship, but he cannot drop the subject of homosexuality: "That [homosexual love] was what the Civil War was about. Abraham Lincoln was a faggot. He was in love with General Grant. So was Jefferson Davis. . . . Sex explains it all. The Colonel's Lady and Judy O'Grady are Lesbians under their skin." By identifying homosexual desire as the cause of all private and public action, a supposedly absurd exaggeration. Bill defuses the tension that expressing his affection for Jake creates. Yet homosexuality is still very much in the air—and "under their skin."

This homosexual current that flows throughout the text reaches its crisis at the same time that the heterosexuality of the text is also at its highest tension: during the liaison that Jake arranges between Brett and Pedro. As I observe, Jake describes Pedro in terms that repeat his descriptions of Brett; further, his first impression of the bullfighter is a physical one—"He was the best-looking boy I have ever seen"—and his later observations continue this focus on Pedro's body. Jake tells Brett that Pedro is "nice to look at," notices his clear, smooth, and very brown skin, and describes Pedro's hand as being "very fine" and his wrist as being "small." Given the way Jake gazes upon Pedro's body, a body that, like Brett's, blends the masculine with the feminine, the moment when Jake brings together Pedro and Brett is also the moment when the text reveals its inability to separate heterosexual from homosexual desire within the desiring body.

This scene has typically been read as the tragic fulfillment of a traditional love triangle in which two men want the same woman and desire moves heterosexually: Jake wants Brett who wants Pedro who wants Brett. Or, as Robert Cohn puts it, Jake becomes Brett's pimp. Yet, given the similarity in the way Jake describes Brett and Pedro, given Jake's homoerotic descriptions of the bullfighter's meeting with the bull, and given the sexual ambiguities that Brett and Jake embody, it seems more accurate to view this relationship not as a triangle but as a web in which desire flows simultaneously in many directions. When Brett and Pedro consummate their desire for each other, Pedro also becomes Jake's surrogate, fulfilling his desire for Brett and hers for him, while Brett becomes Jake's "extension" for satisfying his infatuation with Pedro. Although Jake is physically/phallically absent from Pedro and Brett's "honeymoon," his desire is multiply and symbolically present. Of course, the inadequacy of a figurative presence is disclosed when Brett persists in giving Jake the details about her relationship with Pedro, a verbal reenactment that Jake cannot prevent hearing, even though it drives him to overeat and overdrink.

The final scene of the novel situates Jake between the raised baton of the policeman, an obvious phallic symbol, and the pressure of Brett's body. Such a situation suggests that the novel does not stop trying to bridge the multiple desires of its characters. However, Brett's wishful statement—"we could have had such a damned good time together"—and Jake's ironic question—"Isn't it pretty to think so?"—reveal that at least part of the failure, part of the "lostness" conveyed is that such a bridge cannot be built. The prescriptions for masculinity and femininity and for heterosexuality and homosexuality are too strong to be destroyed or evaded, even in a time and place of sexual and gender experimentation.

Jake and Brett Blur Male-Female Lines

As this analysis suggests, to explore the fundamental equivalences implied during the dancing club scene and to follow their reverberations throughout *The Sun Also Rises* is to construct a network of ambiguities and contradictions pertaining to sexuality and gender. As I admitted above, in creating such a construction, I have had to draw upon the very concepts that I claim Hemingway's novel calls into question (masculinity/femininity, homosexuality/heterosexuality). But by refusing to qualify or resolve the contradictions surrounding these categories and focusing attention upon the points at which they conflict. I have tried to show how Hemingway's novel puts gender and sexuality into constant motion. Although our society attempts to stabilize conduct, appearance, and desire by encoding the first two as masculine or feminine and the latter as homosexual, heterosexual, or bisexual, desire and behavior are not that easily contained and categorized. Actions, appearance, and desire in *The Sun Also Rises* spill over the boundaries of these categories of identity and identification so that the categories become destabilized and collide with one another. The text asks us to suspect, and finally to reject, these systems of representation that are so insufficient and so disabling to efforts to understand human nature.

This is not to say that Brett and Jake have discarded society's scripts for femininity and masculinity, heterosexuality and homosexuality. Their actions, particularly Brett's flirtations and Jake's homophobia, show that they know these scripts well. Nevertheless, as we see by following the several parallels suggested in the club scene, both Jake and Brett continually stray from the lines the scripts demand. That they lack a discourse by which the multiplicity and multifariousness of their desire and conduct can be understood—or understood as "normal"—is society's fault, not their own. But as critics of that society, we must not make this fault of essentializing sexuality and gender our fault too.

Social Issues
in Literature

CHAPTER 3

Contemporary Perspectives on Male and Female Roles

Today's Real Men Are in Touch with Their Feminine Side

Peter Hyman

Peter Hyman, a former Vanity Fair *staffer, journalist, and stand-up comedian, weaves personal anecdotes with social commentary to discuss the recent phenomenon of the urban man who is fully comfortable with the feminine side of his nature. A far cry from the macho Ernest Hemingway hero, the metrosexual is well groomed, well dressed, and somewhat obsessed by fashion and style. Often mistaken for gays, metrosexuals are nevertheless straight.*

The term "metrosexual" was coined in 1994 by Mark Simpson, a British queer theorist who used the word to satirize the phenomenon of "strays"—gay-acting straight men who, with their disposable incomes and consumeristic obsessions, were shopping in record numbers in London. Simpson, however, saw the trend as a self-fulfilling prophecy, created by glossy magazines and their eager sponsors. "Metrosexual man ... is a collector of fantasies about the male sold to him by advertising," he wrote.

It is thus not surprising that metrosexuality's nationwide debut comes via the advertising world. A decade after Simpson's cheeky discovery, Euro RSCG Worldwide a marketing communications conglomerate, surveyed 510 males between the ages of twenty-one and forty-eight on "a battery of issues related to masculinity." Displaying the sort of we-drink-our-own-Kool-Aid sense of smug satisfaction that large marketing entities have mastered, the report declared that there is "an emerging wave of men who chafe against the restrictions of traditional male boundaries" and who "do what they want, buy what they want, enjoy what they want—regardless of whether some people might consider these things unmanly." Chafing? Hmm. How very unmetrosexual of them.

Led by its chief strategy officer, a noted (or at least self-proclaimed) "trend spotter," Euro announced the emergence of a new type of man (not to mention consumer): the metrosexual. This was news to Mr. Simpson, who has suggested that the term probably even predates his original usage. The partial theft of his thunder prompted him to write about his sense of déjà vu, and to question the trend spotter's revelation (corporate trend spotters often "spot" trends well after their legitimate street life has ended, repackaging them for broader consumption without acknowledging their original source; however, the Euro trend spotter apparently called Mr. Simpson sometime later to give him due credit for his "genius," though this attribution does not appear in the Euro report).

Is it possible that the conglomerate that sponsored this study has a vested interest in ensuring that such a class of men exists? And is it thus possible that these results, while generated using legitimate methodologies, are potentially self-serving? For an advertising agency to promote the emergence of a lucrative niche is akin to the semiannual congressional vote on raising the salaries of the members of Congress: it has the imprint of propriety, but at the same time, it lines the pockets of those making the affirmation.

An Urban/Suburban Man

A crucial aspect of metrosexuality, so the name suggests, is geography. Like the yuppie who paved his way, the metrosexual is required to live in *metro*politan areas because this is where all the best shops, salons, and restaurants are located (that this definition may alienate the small but deep-pocketed bands of right-wing neo-Nazis who populate the rural areas of Idaho but who are, no doubt, also fanatical Prada loyalists seems not to be a concern). As it happens, this is also where the money is. While "metropolitan" is loosely defined, I hope it includes the suburban areas that lie outside major cities. If it does not, it ought to, because it is the suburbs where the most help is needed. Men who actually reside in big cities do not have to rely on coaching; they simply need to walk down the street with their eyes open. I have lived in New York City for ten years. I cannot help to have learned a thing or two by osmosis alone, including the habit of always walking on the street side of a woman (to act as a layer of protection should the errant cab careen over the sidewalk. Who says chivalry is dead?).

The New Dandy

The willingness to groom is another hallmark of the metro-sexual, so we are told. But if this is true, then every man who has ever received a hot lather shave is a metrosexual (it came standard with a visit to a corner barber through the 1960s). And since when did proper hygiene become associated with dandyism? Undergoing a luxurious spa treatment on a regular basis may show a willingness to spend money, but it does not imply the making of a new man. Take the Unabomber out of his orange jumper and shackles, trim the beard, toss him into a eucalyptus steam bath for twenty minutes, and he will look good enough to host his own talk show, but I still wouldn't want him sending me holiday care packages in the mail.

Why is metrosexuality happening now? Experts suggest it coincides with an explosion in male vanity—men apparently care more today about the way they look than ever before—which has been gaining momentum for the past fifteen years. To support this contention, they point to Mark Wahlberg's nearly naked appearance in an advertisement for Calvin Klein boxer briefs in the early 1990s, noting that the desire for self-improvement that this ad inspired in straight males was the

The term "metrosexual" refers to a straight man who pays a lot of attention to personal grooming and fashion and exhibits other characteristics commonly associated with gay men. Image copyright Alex Brosa, 2007. Used under license of Shutterstock.com.

flash point for male vanity (never mind that it was aimed at gay men). And what were men doing before that, apart from analyzing baseball statistics, dressing poorly, and lounging on La-Z-Boys in blissful ignorance of their own flabby appearances? Not much, unless one takes into account the history of the world.

The ancient Greeks had some concerns about man's tendency to gaze into reflecting pools, creating mythologies that punished such self-obsession. With his flowing locks and his dream of creating a master race in his own likeness, Alexander the Great was impressed with his, well, greatness (he'd likely be a Kiehl's [skin care] man today, wielding his power to conquer the cosmetics counter at Barneys). And what were the Roman gladiators if not metrosexual men-about-the-Coliseum who wore battle armor instead of Fred Perry tracksuits? [Religious philosopher] Thomas Aquinas, writing in the thirteenth century, saw vanity as pride met with the quest for self-importance (with his friar's haircut and his baggy robes, he might have reached sainthood sooner had he had access to a *Queer Eye* treatment). And [philosopher and political economist] Adam Smith, the baby of this bunch and the author of *Wealth of Nations* (1770), regarded man's desire to make himself distinct as the principle motive for the pursuit of wealth (this at a time when the man on the street wore powdered wigs, makeup, and stockings). With all due respect to Marky Mark's fab abs, male vanity—and the narcissistic practices that it gives rise to—has been around for as long as there have been males.

Relaxing the Manly Code

Metrosexuality, in its highest form, is supposed to represent the freedom for the straight male to tap his creative and sensitive wellsprings, without fear of reprisal. As the rigidly constructed roles regarding masculinity are loosened, these gray-area "feminine" behaviors become more acceptable, and (so the argument goes) men are thus more likely to feel comfortable acting on them. If there is a silver lining to the metrosexual cloud, it is the possibility that, perhaps, American men can finally shed the cloak of he-manliness (waxing their back hair along the way), with Nascar dads embracing *Antiques Roadshow* sons at the food court of an upscale shopping center near you.

But such an ambitious transformation will take more than clever television programming. Moreover, metrosexuality should not be viewed as a magical antidote to homophobia. At best it reflects a modest relaxation of the manly code. There is little reason to believe that a straight man's willingness to co-opt elements of the gay lifestyle (the look, that is) will translate into an honest acceptance of homosexuality and the real-life choices it gives rise to. White America has stolen the best aspects of black culture since before Elvis's gyrations under the banner of multiculturalism, yet racism persists. But unlike the racial and gender equality movements, metrosexuality is not about the legislation of long-overdue rights but rather the freedom from the fear of appearing queer that men bring upon themselves. *The man*, in this case, is men themselves.

Of course, if it were truly acceptable for a straight man to indulge his gay-seeming characteristics without having his sexuality called into question, we would not require a term to describe it. Metrosexuality is simply a hash mark on the continuum of preferences, somewhere between robustly gay and hard-core heterosexual. It has always been there; but advertisers have only just now realized its potency as a marketing credo.

What lies ahead for the metrosexuality agenda? The next logical step for its proponents may be to lobby Congress (as nonmetrosexual a group as exists in any one monument-laden place). Surely the government could be persuaded to enact style-specific laws forcing men to meet certain mandatory requirements in terms of overall body-hair removal, the total allowable number of garments made from synthetic fibers, and dinner-party hosting skills (boot-cut, silhouette-improving Diesel jeans are almost a statutory requirement in certain parts of Manhattan and Los Angeles today). And geneticists are no doubt at work on the Metronome Project, conducting experiments to identify the gay-seeming-but-straight chromosome. Gene splicing will ensure that metrosexuals are born, not made, creating the ultimate captive target audience of loyal shopper clones (like male Stepford wives with extensive lines of credit at Williams-Sonoma and Banana Republic).

From there, metrosexuality could be spun off into globosexuality, an international movement designed to rid the world of pleated pants and machismo. U.N. [United Nations-] sanctioned "style keepers" (trained by members of the ex-East German secret fashion police) would be air-lifted into various hot spots to help bring indigenous communities up to date, showing South American militiamen which outfits work best during a palace coup, helping African tribal leaders select the right wine to go with their next seasonal famine, and providing the Taliban cave dwellers with decorating tips (overhead oil lamps are a no-no! and wall-to-wall dirt floors will not do—or so whine the gay mullahs on *Queer Eye for the Afghani Guy*.)

Until that day, we will just have to have the faith that men (and mankind) can tend to themselves. For despite this long-winded, didactic plea (it's my narcissism, showing itself in the form of wordiness), I don't actually believe that there are that many of my brethren out there who will self-select themselves for inclusion in this group. Metrosexuality seems to be an exclusive club without any members—though anybody still wearing a Members Only jacket with a straight face *might* wish to consider joining, on at least a part-time basis.

Male Conservatism Is Linked to a Fear of Femininity

Stephen J. Ducat

The author, a licensed clinical psychologist and professor of psychology in the School of Humanities at the New College of California, uses a variety of data, including his own research, to prove the central thesis of his book—that the most important thing about being a man is not *being a woman. Stephen J. Ducat argues that the gender gap is about men becoming more conservative, and that there is a direct link between political conservatism and man's fear of being feminine, a condition the author terms "femiphobia." Focusing on four political and social issues—warfare, welfare, the environment, and attitudes toward homosexuality—Ducat contends that men who score as conservative on these issues exhibit what he terms an "anxious masculinity," an unstable male identity based on a repression of the feminine. Ducat finds that the events of September 11, 2001, have led to heightened appreciation for machismo, and he gives several examples from politics and culture.*

White privilege isn't what it used to be—especially if you're a working-class male. Median annual wages for blue-collar men went down by 11.5 percent between 1979 and 1995, according to the Labor Department. Since then, as a result of global trade agreements and the consequent export of manufacturing plants, industrial jobs have been steadily hemorrhaging from the United States. From the time [George W.] Bush assumed the presidency in 2000, the nation has lost nearly five million jobs—the bulk of which have been in manufacturing. Seventy-five percent of the positions that *are* available as of this writing are low-wage service sector jobs.

Stephen J. Ducat, "Voting Like a Man: The Psychodynamics of the Gender Gap in Political Attitudes," *The Wimp Factor*, Boston: Beacon Press, 2004, pp. 168–230. Copyright © 2004 by Stephen J. Ducat. All rights reserved. Reprinted by permission of Beacon Press, Boston.

The president's tax cuts not only provide the greatest relief to the wealthy, but working-class families are going to suffer consequences from which the economic elite are immune, such as declining revenues for public schools. . . .

This decline in the economic and physical well-being of blue-collar workers has been largely, though not exclusively, the result of explicit Republican governing philosophy and practice. Since none of these facts is garnered from classified sources, one would expect that the majority of white working-class men, acting in their own obvious material self-interest, would be firmly opposed to GOP [Grand Old Party, a nickname for the Republican Party] candidates. The reality of current public opinion, however, sits in stark contrast to such an expectation. A survey conducted in December of 2003 by the Pew Research Center for the People and the Press found that non-college-educated white men preferred George W. Bush to a Democrat in the 2004 election by 60 percent to 25 percent. An ABC/*Washington Post* poll revealed that white men in general were inclined to vote for Bush over an unnamed Democrat by 62 percent to 29 percent, an astonishing 30 percent margin, while white women preferred a Democrat by a small margin. The Pew survey found that men without college degrees actually supported Bush more than did men who had graduated from college. . . . [The question remains]: How could a majority or even a plurality of working-class men ever have endorsed a politician who has played such a central role in their loss of well-being and security?

The gender gap in political attitudes and voting behavior began after Ronald Reagan, the founding father of the Republican Revolution, ascended to power in 1980—precisely the period that marked the most precipitous decline in the economic status of working-class men. This makes the political history of the last two and a half decades seem even more startlingly counterintuitive: as men's wages went down, their conservatism went up. The more the Republican agents of the economic elite made the life of white male workers difficult, the more these men flocked to the GOP. Those inclined to interpret this paradox as simply an expression of political naivete and ignorance, secondary to the center-right bias of the corporate media, might be discomfited to know the results of a study conducted by the Roper Center for Public Opinion Research on the Bush tax cut. Among the poorest blue-collar men (with incomes of thirty thousand dollars or less) who *agreed* with the statement that "this tax plan benefits mainly the rich," 53 percent nevertheless favored it. In contrast, only 35 percent of those in the seventy-five thousand dollar income bracket favored the tax cut, in spite of believing that the wealthy were the main beneficiaries. How can we make sense of what looks like an astonishing display of economic irrationality if not masochism?

The sociologist Arlie Hochschild, in an insightful article that addresses precisely this issue, argues that what the Republicans in general and the Bush administration in particular have so skillfully finessed is the methodical engineering of displaced rage. She notes that the anger of working-class men has been effectively "directed downward—at 'welfare cheats,' women, gays, blacks, and immigrants," outward "at alien enemies," and definitely away from "job exporters and rich tax dodgers." Hochschild also describes the Republicans' facile exploitation of the fear and vulnerability generated not only by economic insecurity but by the uncertainties and pervasive sense of threat that characterizes the post-9/11 world. As she describes the situation, "George W. Bush is deregulating American global capitalism with one hand while regulating the feelings it produces with the other. Or, to put it another way, he is doing nothing to change the causes of fear, and everything to channel the feeling and expression of it."

Although I would not take issue with Hochschild's trenchant formulation there is one question that could be addressed more fully. Why men? Why are males particularly susceptible to this manipulation? While men in general tend to vote Republican, I started this chapter looking at the conservatism of *working-class* men precisely because it seemed the most counterintuitive. In other words, it defies the conventional wisdom that economic self-interest is the primary driving force in shaping political allegiances. It does seem that the right-wing tendencies of blue-collar men militate against a simple economic motive for the gender gap, and highlight the role of *masculinity* in the political disparities between men and women.

That said, class and gender can be slippery categories, and at times exchangeable with one another. For example, to be a subordinate, to have others "on top," is often construed by members of a patriarchal culture as assuming a feminine position. So, even though notions of blue-collar manhood are saturated with fantasies of primitive muscularity, this is in tension with the "feminizing" experience of being at the bottom in an economic hierarchy, or at the lowest rung in a workplace command structure. In addition, regardless of the significant presence of women in the labor market, masculinity is often defined in terms of a man's capacity to be a provider—a position that is far more likely to be precarious for working-class men, given their lower wages and their vulnerability to underemployment and job loss. (While the focus here is on some of the ways that class positions get *gendered*, it should be noted that gender can also be a *class* position, the major manifestation being patriarchy itself—the distribution of power, resources, and privilege based on maleness.)

There is another way that class can morph into gender. [There is a] tradition in American politics of equating certain expressions of luxury and upper-class comfort with effeminacy. While this was a problem for the Republicans during the reign of George Herbert Walker Bush, the faux-populism of the Bush II regime and their allies seems to have convinced many men that it is the *left* that drips with the effete accoutrements of feminizing wealth. Conservative talk shows are filled with denunciations of "latte liberals" and the "Volvo-driving, *New-York-Times*-reading liberal elite." This rhetoric, combined with the regular-guy persona of George W. Bush—his inarticulateness and anti-intellectual presentation—has successfully disguised the president's own patrician roots. One of Bush's more shrewd performances, widely denounced at the time, was his joke during a speech at Yale, his alma mater, that his success proves you can get a C—average and still become president. But, as important as these considerations of class may be, it should not be forgotten that the gender gap involves men of all economic strata, making the role of masculinity the most important factor in understanding the growing political chasm that now divides men and women.

In Bed with the Opposition

Within days after the 2000 election, newspapers across the United States printed color-coded maps in red and blue to denote, respectively, the states that went Republican and those that voted Democratic. This visual aid also highlighted the stark political divisions in the country, especially the radically disparate values that constitute the psychological borders between America's various geographical regions. If reporters had wanted to give a more detailed picture of the fault lines that separate citizens from one another, they could have created a different color-coded portrait of the nation, one divided between *pink* and blue. For the first time since the election of Ronald Reagan in 1980, women and men, as distinct groups, elected different candidates—most women voted for [Al] Gore, while the vast majority of men selected Bush. Of course, this sort of division would not have lent itself well to a national map because the political fissures in many cases would have run right down the center of middle-class bedrooms. This is even truer now than it was then. In a recent survey conducted by Democratic pollster Celinda Lake, married voters were asked if their partners had chosen the same candidates that they did. Half the women said "no," in contrast to only a quarter of the men. Lake's understanding of the discrepancy is that the women were reluctant to disabuse their husbands of their fantasy of political agreement. "We call it the 'Sure, honey' factor," Lake explains. It appears that the more educated a woman is, the more likely she is to disagree with her husband politically, and thus favor Democratic candidates. According to a *USA Today*/CNN/Gallup poll conducted between January and November of 2003, the gender gap among those with a high-school diploma or less was 10 percent. For college graduates it jumped to twenty percentage points, while the gap became a gulf for voters who had taken postgraduate courses, leaping to 28 percent. . . .

Why Can't a Liberal Be More Like a Man?

One thing is clear: the gender gap has been driven by men's growing conservatism, not by women's liberalism. This was noted as far back as 1996 by Everett C. Ladd of the Roper Center, who said. "In truth; women are not really more Democratic than they were fifteen years ago. It's that men have become more Republican." Since women's support is more equally divided among the two parties, the net benefit goes to Republicans. Since men are the ones who have changed, it is the *male* side of the political divide that most urgently calls for an explanation. In other words, if we can understand the dynamics behind male conservatism, we will be in a much better position to make sense of the dramatic lurch to the right that has marked the last two and a half decades—because to a certain extent they are the same phenomenon.

Just prior to the 2000 election, the *Los Angeles Times* interviewed a young man who summarized his impression of the two main candidates: "Bush is a guy's guy. He's from Texas, so he's more of a he-man, leatherneck type. . . . Gore, he's sensitive. He's supposed to be for the environment. He's always talking about kids and families." While not offering the most nuanced analysis, this man effectively illustrates two key components of political thinking that inform the gender gap for men: an assessment of the masculinity of a candidate, and a perception, however unconscious, that certain issues or political stances are gendered. In this example, the two are linked— the supposedly unmanly candidate is naturally taken up with "feminine" issues like the environment and concern for children. In some ways these two components are hard to disentangle. A male politician with a hypermasculine image, who (temporarily) possesses the phallus, can sometimes masculinize an issue that might otherwise have a feminine cast, at least enough to have his view prevail. Lyndon Johnson, a manly hawk on the Vietnam War, had enough phallic "street cred" when it came to battling Southern racists and supporting the issue of racial equality, a cause which even today is of much greater concern to women than men. . . .

[There] remain profound differences between men and women on a wide range of issues. My own research . . . found that men are more likely than women to take the typical conservative position on military intervention . . . , environmental protection, the caretaking functions of the state (such as Welfare), and homosexuality. . . .

In my own research on the gender gap, which I conducted using 294 subjects (140 males and 154 females) after the first Iraq war and before the second one, men were much more likely to endorse statements that linked military victory with one's own self-esteem. For example, significantly more men than women strongly agreed with the statements "When I saw our powerful American forces on TV 'kick Iraqi butt' during the Persian Gulf War, I too felt powerful," and "Seeing our President stand up to America's enemies, in some ways makes me feel like I stand taller." This might help explain the results reported by another researcher who studied the gender gap in attitudes toward the Persian Gulf War. She found that not only did far more men support the war, but their support was only minimally affected by the changing goals of the military operation. Conversely, women's favorable view of the war changed considerably, as the stated ends shifted. . . .

And, we should not overlook the obvious—defeating an enemy is, more than anything else, an expression of *domination*, which . . . is the bottom-line criterion for masculinity in nearly all patriarchal cultures. The link between domination and manhood has also been confirmed by empirical studies. Several researchers have found that men exhibit a greater "social dominance orientation" than women, which leads them to hold a variety of anti-egalitarian positions. In particular, males, in contrast to females, are not only more likely to be pro-war but are also more comfortable with racial and class inequities. It does seem likely that dominance, whether vicarious or direct, may be a primary motivation for men to support war, and at times may underlie more lofty and principled rationalizations. "Operation Kiss My Ass" does sound far less exalted than "Operation Iraqi Freedom" but would probably poll well, at least among, men. . . .

Male Conservatism: The Big Picture

[Men] are much more likely than women to hold right-wing views on a number of major political issues. I have chosen to look closely at the gender gap in only four of these areas—warfare, the caretaking functions of government, environmental protection, and homophobia—largely because these were the primary issues covered in my own research, and in so doing I was able to establish some interesting correlations. . . . Not surprisingly, the men who scored in the conservative direction on one of these four issues were also conservative on the other three. And . . . , on all the issues, men were significantly more likely than women to embrace the right-wing position. Perhaps the most notable findings, and those that to my knowledge have not been assessed by other researchers, were the positive correlations between male conservatism and measures that assessed fear of men's feminity and gender role conflict.

The male subjects in my study were much more likely than the females to be made uneasy by the prospect of a man doing something stereotypically feminine. Those men who held the most conservative positions were also the ones to evince the greatest concern about not being like a woman. My study only established a correlation, not a causal relationship, between fear of men's feminity (femiphobia) and political conservatism. Nevertheless, because gender identity and gender role socialization developmentally precede the formation of abstract concepts such as political ideology, it seems likely that if one of these variables were causal it would be femiphobia.

At first thought, it would seem most objective and fair-minded to regard the conservative political views more typical of men as merely one point on a continuum of equally reasonable ideas, no more or less healthy, valid, or problematic than liberal or progressive beliefs. However, the correlation between adherence to right-wing ideology and male gender role conflict make it difficult to view men's conservatism with such relativistic equanimity. To score high on the measure of gender role conflict administered to my subjects means that one tends to have chronic anxieties about personal achievement, competence, failure, and career and financial success. Such a man is also more likely to be preoccupied with attaining dominance over others. In addition, he is likely to experience a severe constriction in his ability to express any positive emotions toward other males. In other studies, high scores on the measure of gender role conflict used in my research have been positively correlated with sexual coercion, hostility toward women, impaired intimacy, negative attitudes toward help seeking, low self-esteem, marital dissatisfaction, depression, anxiety, authoritarian personality style, general psychological distress, and some of the most extreme manifestations of paranoia, psychotic thinking, and obsessive-compulsive behavior. This may seem like a harsh assessment, but a recent study of the psychological correlates of political conservatism paints an equally discouraging view. . . .

The Phallus Rises from the Ashes

In spite of a new and pervasive sense of vulnerability occasioned by the horrific events of September 11 [2001], the phallic associations to the towers were insistently retained by many Americans. In New York City, a flyer was distributed that featured an image of Osama bin Laden being anally raped by the World Trade Center. The accompanying caption read, "You like skyscrapers, bitch?" Even the planned memorial replacement for the destroyed monoliths was referred to by the *New York Post* as the "Power Tower."

There were other, more profound, ways in which the terrorist attacks provided America with an opportunity for cultural remasculinization. First, it facilitated the revivification of "heroic" manhood, by turning altruistic New York firemen, policemen, and assorted male volunteers into iconic rescue-worker hunks, signposts of a new era of defeminized men (who could still, however, be sensitive enough to cry over tragic losses). A month and a half after the attacks, a *New York Times* headline announced, "Heavy Lifting Required: The Return of Manly Men." The article is flanked by a photo of a group of burly male rescue workers and soldiers, studly and uniformed. The caption emphasized the performative aspects of the phenomenon these men supposedly represented: "The attacks of Sept. 11 have brought more than a few good men back into the cultural limelight." Nevertheless, their serious, world-weary expressions and grimy clothing made it clear they were *not* The Village People [disco group].

Among the many product tie-ins to this trend was a "2003 Calendar of Heroes" featuring twelve specimens of bare-chested firefighter beefcake. The man on the cover is posed in front of the Empire State Building, now the tallest structure in New York. The photo is framed so as to establish a kind of equivalence between the firefighter and the phallic monument—the former positioned on the left, and the latter on the right, making them appear to be about the same size.

The August 2002 headline for a column penned by conservative pundit James R. Pinkerton proclaimed, "Real Men Back in Style." He quotes grizzled coal miners, whose first request upon being rescued is, "We need some chew." Pinkerton then leaps from this anecdote to a cornball homage to post-9/11 revitalized machismo: "Chewing tobacco? That's men for you, fraternal enough to save lives, macho enough to be jaunty in the face of death, manly enough to be politically incorrect. Male virtues and values have never really changed, but after decades of disdain, Americans are seeing the natural ways of men in a new and more positive light." Even pencil-necked white-collar workers, "those with the softest hands," suffer from that "atavistic yearning to recapture the sweaty, risky ways of the past."

This celebration of recovered masculinity reached all the way to the fashion runways of Milan and Paris, where hulking male models sported the latest in commando chic, camouflage muscle shirts, combat fatigues festooned with cartridge belts, and cowboy clothes. Stefano Tonchi, of *Esquire* magazine, seemed to understand what was at stake in the cowboy designs of Tom Ford, the creative director of Gucci, and a Texan: "For Tom, the western theme is about going back to his roots." Moreover, "with cowboys, there is also less gender confusion. Cowboys are not girly." So, it seems that behind even this festive heralding of the new manhood there lurked the old femiphobic anxiety.

These developments dovetailed perfectly with a pre-9/11 mass culture trend—World War II nostalgia. According to the avalanche of books and films idealizing the "good war" and the men who fought it, this period was supposedly a time of unambivalent and secure masculinity, in which gender and other aspects of cultural life were not plagued by uncertainty and conflict. Such nostalgia was ripe for harvesting by boosters for the new Republican national security state, particularly in its domestic and global war without end against real and imagined terrorist threats. One place where a link was established between the sanitized vision of the past and the present cultural moment was in the variety of soft-focus analyses of George W. Bush's putative transformation from a callow frat boy to a mature leader whose commanding presence now approached the manly gravitas of the "greatest generation." Not surprisingly, such claims were heard frequently on right-wing talk radio. But, even centrist, middle-of-the-road media echoed this perception, though it was expressed with a bit less enthusiasm. For example, a writer for *USA Today* said, "Bush has told advisors that he believes confronting the enemy is a chance for him and his fellow baby boomers to refocus their lives and prove they have the same kind of valor and commitment their fathers showed in WWII." In a *New York Times* op-ed column, David Frum, a Republican speechwriter, delivered an expectable piece of partisan puffery on Mr. Bush, chiefly notable for "staying on message" (as political consultants often counsel) regarding the new improved post-9/11 chief executive. "Today," Frum announced, "Mr. Bush is more than a strong president: he dominates his own party in a way that few modern presidents ever have." Should the reader have any difficulty discerning the point, the column is accompanied by a visual aid—a cartoon with a "W" branding iron in the foreground and a herd of elephants bearing the "W" brand on their hindquarters in the background. Domination, for contemporary politicians, no less than for those in ancient Greece, remains the defining criterion for masculinity.

The prize for the most gushing, over-the-top encomium to post-9/11 revivified manhood has to go to the special issue of

The American Enterprise, entitled "Real Men: They're Back." This delirious right-wing strut-fest defies parody, and contains inspirational articles such as "The Return of Manly Leaders and the Americans Who Love Them," "Why We Need Macho Men," "The Car and the Man," "Me Man, Me Hunt!" and, in case you thought they couldn't get more redundant, "The Manliness of Men:" The best feature, however, is surely the "research" article, "Indicators," which displays a number of graphs that compare the manliness of Republican and Democratic male members of Congress. Endeavoring to be as scientific as possible, the authors developed objective criteria, such as whether the congressman in question had ever been a hunter ("successfully bagged an animal more than once"), a mechanic ("performed extensive mechanical work on a motor vehicle"), a spy ("operative in any intelligence service"), or an Eagle Scout. While they grudgingly acknowledge that an equal number of Democrats and Republicans had been firefighters and policemen, those professions are left off the chart titled "GOP-GUY."

It might be instructive to point out an obvious, but never discussed, logical implication of all this talk about a recovered masculinity: where there is a sense of something having been refound, there must have been a prior experience of loss. . . . Male identity will always be an unstable psychological achievement, as long as it is based on repression—on the disavowal of whatever is construed as feminine. From my experience as a clinical psychologist, I have learned that repression does not enable people to get rid of anything; it only helps them remain clueless about its presence. Thus, the discourse of the "new" post-9/11 machismo can be read as an indication of something that has felt *absent* or at least imperiled, as much as it is about something temporarily recovered.

The Death of Feminism

Maureen Dowd

In this controversial work, the title of which is a twist on E.B. White and James Thurber's humorous 1929 work, Is Sex Necessary?, *the author assesses the state of feminism forty years after the birth of the women's movement and the sexual revolution of the 1960s. She argues that while there were some triumphs in the early days of the women's movement, the backlash against women has lasted for forty years. At the dawn of feminism, Dowd contends many women believed they could have it all, while today's woman recognizes life is about complicated choices. In this excerpt, she uses witty examples from her own life to argue that men are threatened by successful women. She also accuses today's women of being more concerned with their appearance than with matters of substance. Dowd is a* New York Times *op-ed columnist. She won the 1999 Pulitzer Prize for Distinguished Commentary for her columns on the impeachment of President Bill Clinton.*

I don't understand men.

I don't even understand what I don't understand about men.

They're a most inscrutable bunch, really.

I had a moment of dazzling clarity when I was twenty-seven; a rush of confidence that I had cracked the code. But it was, alas, an illusion.

I think I overcomplicated their simplicity. Or oversimplified their simplicity. Are they as complicated as a pile of wood? Or as simple as a squid?

I was loath to accept the premise of [comedian] Jerry Seinfeld, who claims that "men are really nothing more that extremely advanced dogs" who want the same thing from their women that they want from their underwear: "A little bit of support and a little bit of freedom."

The Jazz Age

I was more prone to go with the thesis of James Thurber and E. B. White in their seminal 1929 treatise, *Is Sex Necessary?*, that the American male was the least understood of all male animals, and that more attention needed to be paid to his complexity—"the importance of what he is thinking about and what he intends to do, or at least what he would like to do. . . .

"How often do you hear it said that the little whims and desires of a man should be cherished, or even listened to? You don't hear it said at all. What you do hear is that 'the way to a man's heart is through his stomach.' A thing like that hardens a man. He may eat his spinach and say nothing, but he is being hardened just the same."

Thurber and White don't date the start of the troubles between men and women to the snaky Eve.

They contend that things got bollixed up in the 1920s, when the female, "face-to-face with the male's simple desire to sit down and hold her" (aka "the attack of the male"), retaliated with irritating Diversion Subterfuges—such as Fudge Making and Indoor Games for groups—meant to fend off and put Man in his place.

"The American male's repugnance to charades, which is equaled, perhaps, by his repugnance to nothing at all, goes back to those years," the authors explained.

I know women are disorienting to men, too.

In his memoir about *The New Yorker, The Years with Ross*, Thurber tells this story from the early '50s about the legendary editor's reaction to having a baby girl:

"One morning, I found Ross, worried and stoop-shouldered, pacing a corridor, jingling those pocket coins. He came right out with his current anxiety. 'Goddamn it. I can't think of any *man* that has a daughter. I think of men as having boys, and women as having girls.'

"'I have a daughter,' I said, 'and I wanted a daughter.'

"'That's not natural, is it?' he demanded. 'I never heard of a man that didn't want a son. Can you name any, well, you know, goddamn it—terribly masculine men with daughters?'

"The sun and moon of reassurance shone in his face when I came up with Jack Dempsey [world heavyweight boxing champion, who] has two children, both girls.' His day was saved from the wreckage of despair, but he still had one final depressed world. 'Goddamn it. I hate the idea of going around with female hormones in me.'"

In the final analysis, Thurber and White decided matters went irretrievably awry during the Jazz Age when flappers began to imitate men, smoking, drinking, wanting to earn money ("not much, but some") and thinking they had "the right to be sexual." All these strained attempts at equality, they contend, destroyed the mystery of the sexual tango, or sexual Charleston, if you will.

This spurt of cocky independence faded, and over the decades women lapsed back into domesticity and deference, until their only avatars were perfect gingham moms such as Donna Reed, June Cleaver and Harriet Nelson [mothers in 1950s television shows].

The Sexual Revolution

Then came the Sexual Revolution. When I entered college, in 1969, women were bursting out of their '50s chrysalis. The Jazz Age spirit flared in the Age of Aquarius. Women were once again imitating men and acting all independent: smoking, drinking, wanting to earn money (not as much, but some) and thinking the Pill gave them "the right to be sexual."

I didn't fit in with the brazen new world of hard-charging feminists. I was more of a fun-loving (if chaste) Carrie Bradshaw type [TV character in *Sex and the City*], a breed that wouldn't come into vogue for several more decades.

I hated the dirty, unisex jeans and no-makeup look and drugs that zoned you out, and I couldn't understand the appeal of dances that didn't involve touching your partner.

In the universe of Eros, I longed for style and wit. I loved the Art Deco glamour of '30s movies. I wanted to dance the Continental like Fred [Astaire] and Ginger [Rogers] in white hotel suites; drink martinis like Myrna Loy and William Powell; live the life of a screwball heroine like Katharine Hepburn, wearing a gold lame gown cut on the bias, cavorting with Cary Grant, strolling along Fifth Avenue with my pet leopard.

My mom would just shake her head and tell me that my idea of the '30s was wildly romanticized. "We were poor," she'd say. "We didn't dance around in white hotel suites."

I took the idealism and passion of the '60s for granted, simply assuming we were sailing toward perfect equality with men, a utopian world at home and at work.

I didn't listen to my mom when she advised me to get a suitcase with wheels before my first trip to Europe. I didn't listen to her before my first cocktail party, when she told me that men prefer homemade dinner rolls stuffed with turkey and ham to expensive catered goose pâté and exotic cheese wheels. "Simplicity pays," she said smugly, when all the guys swarmed around her sandwiches.

And I didn't listen to her when she cautioned me about the chimera of equality.

On my thirty-first birthday, she sent me a bankbook with a modest nest egg she had saved for me. "I always felt that the girls in a family should get a little more than the boys even though all are equally loved," she wrote in a letter. "They need a little cushion to fall back on. Women can stand on the Empire State Building and scream to the heavens that they are equal to men and liberated, but until they have the same anatomy, it's a lie. It's more of a man's world today than ever. Men can eat their cake in unlimited bakeries."

I thought she was just being Old World, like my favorite jade, [writer] Dorothy Parker, when she wrote:

By the time you're his,

Shivering and sighing,

And he vows his passion is

Infinite, undying—

Lady, make a note of this:

One of you is lying.

I thought the struggle for egalitarianism was a cinch, so I could leave it to my earnest sisters in black turtlenecks and Birkenstocks. I figured there was plenty of time for me to get serious later, that America would always be full of passionate and full-throated debate about the big stuff—social issues, sexual equality, civil rights—rather than tinny right-left food fights and shrieking conservative babes with blond hair, long legs and miniskirts going on TV to trash women and women's rights. . . .

Little did I realize that the sexual revolution would have the unexpected consequence of intensifying the confusion between the sexes, leaving women in a tangle of dependence and independence as they entered the twenty-first century. The fewer the barriers, the more muddied the waters. It never occurred to me that the more women aped men, in everything from dress to orgasms, the more we would realize how inalienably different the sexes are.

Or, most curious of all, that women would move from playing with Barbie to denouncing Barbie to remaking themselves as Barbie.

Maybe we should have known that the story of women's progress would be more of a zigzag than a superhighway, that the triumph of feminism would last a nanosecond while the backlash lasted forty years.

And that all the triumphant moments of feminism—from the selection of Geraldine Ferraro [vice presidential candidate on the Democratic Party ticket in 1984] to the Anita Hill hearings [in which she accused Supreme Court Justice nominee Clarence Thomas of sexual harassments during his senate confirmation hearings] to the co-presidency of buy-one-get-one-free First Lady Hillary Rodham Clinton—would unleash negative reactions toward women.

Despite the best efforts of philosophers, politicians, historians, novelists, screenwriters, linguists, therapists, anthropologists and facilitators, men and women are still in a muddle in the boardroom, the Situation Room and the bedroom. . . .

The entanglements between men and women come in three forms: tragedies, comedies and tragicomedies. Outrage regularly alternates with silliness. Illusions are often more interesting than realities. Causes and desires are regularly mixed up. Will there ever be peace? I doubt it. But there should always be laughter.

My mom, a soft touch who loved men, suggested that I change my title to *Why Men Are Necessary.* "Men *are* necessary for breeding and heavy lifting," she said wryly.

But, difficult as it is, we must face up to the tough questions. As a species, it's possible that men are ever so last century. Are they any longer necessary for procreation? Have they proven themselves emotionally incapable of governing the country because they are really the ones subject to hissy fits and hormonal imbalances? Is their pillaging and plundering, war-mongering, empire-building Y chromosome melting faster than the Wicked Witch of the West? Is it time to dispense with all those oxygen-depleting men batting out opinions in newspapers, TV and blogs, and those computer-generated-looking male anchor clones on network news?

The Plastic Revolution

And what about women? Are we regressing? Or advancing along the winding scenic route in ways we hadn't predicted? I'm continually astonished, provoked and flummoxed by the odd and stunning trajectory men and women have traveled from the big bang of the Sexual Revolution to the big busts of the Plastic Revolution.

The free-love idea that sex could be casual and safe and unfraught was, in retrospect, chuckleheaded. As my friend Leon Wieseltier, the literary editor for *The New Republic*, observes: "Sex is a spiritual obligation. It makes up for the poverty of bourgeois experience. We're too late for the Spanish Civil War. We missed the landing at Omaha Beach [during World War II]. But still we need to know what we're capable of. So it is in the realm of private life that we have to risk ourselves, to disclose ourselves, to vindicate ourselves; and the more private, the more illuminating. Our theater of self-discovery is smaller. And in this lucky but shrunken theater the bedroom looms very large. It is the front line, the foxhole.

"The bedroom is where people who live otherwise safe lives can learn how cowardly or courageous they are, what their deepest and most dangerous desires are, whether they can follow the unreason within them to what it, too, can teach. [Leo] Tolstoy said that modern tragedy should be set in the bedroom."

If [feminist] Gloria Steinem had had a crystal ball and flashed forward to a 2005 filled with catfights and women scheming to trap men, snag the coveted honorific "Mrs.," get cosmetic procedures to look like Playmate bombshells and dress, as Dave Chappelle says, like "whores" would the sister have even bothered to lead that bonfire of the brass?

I think not.

Whether or not American feminism will be defeated by American conservatism it is incontrovertibly true that American feminism was trumped by American narcissism.

This is a season when the female beau ideal is not Gloria Steinem a serious bunny but Jessica Simpson a simple bunny, and when Hollywood's remake of *The Stepford Wives* stumbled because it was no longer satire but documentary.

I had to live through disco pointy polyester shirt collars greed is good, me decade, yuppie consumerism and cigar bars—coming full circle from platform shoes and Diane von Furstenberg wrap dresses to platform shoes and Diane von Furstenberg wrap dresses—before I was hit with a pang of nostalgia for the opportunity I'd missed in college.

We would never again be so consumed with changing the world. The more time passed, the more Americans simply focused on changing themselves. We've become a nation of Frankensteins and our monster is us. With everyone working so hard at altering their facades, we no longer have natural selection. We have unnatural selection.

Emma Woodhouse [Jane Austen's heroine in the novel *Emma*] learned the hard way about the dangers of makeovers. She tried to turn her simple friend, Harriet Smith, into a girl with airs and aspirations. Too late, Jane Austen's heroine realized that she had altered Harriet for the worse, from humble to vain. Literature is rife with cautionary tales about experiments in identity—from Dorian Gray to Jay Gatsby to Tom Ripley whose murderous motto was: "Better a fake somebody than a real nobody."

But our contemporary carnival of makeovers does not concern itself with virtue, only vanity. We have grown superficial even about surfaces. The whole country seems to have embraced Oscar Wilde's teaching that "It is only the shallow who do not judge by appearance." The national obsession with appearance is a chronicle of social psychosis straight out of [science fiction writer] Philip K. Dick. . . .

I came of age in interlocking male institutions: My dad was a police detective, I was in the Catholic Church and I had three brothers. The nation's capital we lived in was peppered with statues honoring men. When I first got into journalism, I covered sports, then politics, at a time when they were even more male-dominated arenas.

Along the way, I got into the habit of tweaking the oppressors. I imagined that women were forever destined to a life of dissidence.

Though the science is mainly of metaphorical interest to me—a fascinating biological parable—the new research into sex chromosomes suggests that all that antler crashing over the centuries has tuckered out the Y. Men are now the weaker sex geneticists say and could soon disappear altogether—taking March Madness and cold pizza in the morning with them.

Only another hundred thousand years—or ten million, if you believe the Y optimists—and the male chromosome could go the way of the dial up connection.

So dear readers of the soon-to-be-extinct male persuasion you're on notice.

In the year 102,005 or 10,002,005 at the latest we'll finally have our fair share of female network anchors, female priests, female columnists, female Supreme Court justices, corrupt female CEOs [chief executive officers] and philandering female presidents.

And we'll run the world.

In a manly way of course.

A Defense of Manliness

Harvey C. Mansfield

Harvey C. Mansfield is the William R. Kenan Jr. professor of government at Harvard University. He won a National Humanities Medal in 2004. He has written numerous scholarly works on such philosophers as Aristotle, Edmund Burke, and Alexis de Tocqueville. In 1997, in a controversial op-ed column for the Wall Street Journal, *Mansfield wrote that the "protective element of manliness is endangered by women having equal access to jobs outside the home." In the book from which this excerpt is taken, he expands on his theme of manliness. Although slightly moderating his earlier views, Mansfield argues that the gender-neutral society in fact doesn't exist—that men still hold more traditionally male jobs, while women hold more traditionally female jobs. Manly men—in the tradition of actor John Wayne, President Harry S. Truman, and the New York City policemen and firemen on September 11, 2001—are confident and have an ability to command; they are assertive and willing to risk their lives to save a life. Manliness in Mansfield's view, imbues men with nobility.*

What is [manliness]? It's best to start from examples we know: our sports heroes, too many to name; Margaret Thatcher, the British prime minister who is the mightiest woman of our time (What! a woman, manly?); Harry S. Truman, who said "the buck stops here"; Humphrey Bogart, who as Rick in *Casablanca* was confident and cynical—cool before "cool" was invented; and the courageous police and firemen in New York City on September 11, 2001. Manliness seeks and welcomes drama and prefers times of war, conflict, and risk. Manliness brings change or restores order at moments when routine is not enough, when the plan fails, when the whole idea of rational control by modern science develops leaks. Manliness is the next-to-last resort, before resignation and prayer.

We today inhabit a society with a very new justice, long overdue: the gender-neutral society. In this new society your sex does not determine your rights, your duties, or your place. The gender-neutral society regards sex as an irrational hindrance to freedom because it subordinates women to men, and to efficiency because it misuses their abilities. Manliness, the quality, mostly of one sex, gets in the way of an equal or reasonable distribution of tasks and rewards; it seems to promote a bias in favor of men over women. . . .

Manliness Is Assertiveness and *Thumos*

Manliness is something that affects us all, sometimes that most anyone can see. Common sense has a lot to say about it. For the most part, I take the side of common sense. I like its forthright defense of stereotypes regarding the sexes. I am not so friendly to the two sciences that treat manliness, social psychology, and evolutionary biology, even though they, too, largely support those stereotypes. The evidence the social psychologists compile on the differences between the sexes is useful for refuting those who deny sex differences or regard them as easily changed, and there is fascination in being shown small but significant differences in the ways that men and women do the same things in daily life. These differences are observable by anyone who cares to look and available in the stereotypes of common sense, but it is reassuring to see science catch up with truth and confirm in interesting ways what we already know.

On the whole, however, I am quite critical of the scientific understanding of manliness, whether in social psychology or evolutionary biology. These sciences see manliness at its lowest as aggression and altogether fail to consider the phenomenon of manly assertiveness. A manly man asserts himself so that he and the justice he demands are not overlooked. He rouses himself and seeks attention for what he deems important, sometimes something big—in the case of the New York uniforms and the Islamic fascists, the nature and value of Western civilization. These sciences, and science generally, are uncomfortable in the presence of big questions of human importance like this one. This is a severe limitation for the study of manliness that I cannot accept.

And science does not even understand aggression correctly or fully because it is completely ignorant of the phenomenon of *thumos*, known to Plato and Aristotle but later abandoned because it was inconvenient to the agenda of modern science. *Thumos* is a quality of spiritedness, shared by humans and animals, that induces humans, and especially manly men, to risk their lives in order to save their lives. That's a paradox familiar to all human beings who ever get angry. But it is a fact almost unknown in the scientific literature on manliness. As manliness is made out of that paradox, it is, to say the least, more complicated than the simplistic drives of aggression, domination, and self-presentation to which science tries to reduce manliness. I have done my best to develop assertiveness and *thumos* as features of manliness, and my book—here's an example of a manly assertion—is the only ready-to-hand treatment of manliness in these two respects and as a whole that you will find. . . .

Today the very word *manliness* seems quaint and obsolete. We are in the process of making the English language gender-neutral, and manliness, the quality of one gender, or rather, of one sex, seems to describe the essence of the enemy we are attacking, the evil we are eradicating. . . .

A Definition of Gender Neutrality

The attempt to make our language gender-neutral reveals something of the ambition of our democracy today. A gender-neutral language implies a gender-neutral society, marking a pervasive change in the way we live our lives. Our society has adopted, quite without realizing the magnitude of the change, a practice of equality between the sexes that has never been known before in all human history. The principle of equality, born in modern times, is several centuries old, but as its application to the sexes is very new, we can see that even democratic peoples were long content to ignore very obvious inequality between the sexes. That inconsistency is no longer accepted. Much more has occurred, and is yet under way, than a mere adjustment of law to ensure equal access of women to jobs. Some women want a law of affirmative action to give them an advantage in competitive situations from which they have been so long excluded, and for which they may not be prepared. But that adjustment—not accepted by all women—is considered temporary and transitional even by its advocates. New attitudes are recommended, new behavior is required, if only to sustain such a law and make it work. The long-term goal, however far in the future, is gender neutrality. Now what does that mean?

Let me try to fashion an answer from diverse strands of present-day thinking, keeping things simple for now. Gender neutrality in theory is abstracting from sexual differences so as to make jobs and professions (especially the latter) open to both sexes. Wherever your sex used to determine your opportunities, it must now be seen as irrelevant. How can you regard sex as irrelevant when it used to be considered highly relevant? The answer is that one must oppose the traditional thinking and "raise consciousness" as to what women can or ought to do. To overcome prejudice against women, they must be said and shown to be equal to men. It is not enough merely to set aside sexual differences. That is the principle. But since the new principle, like everything new in morals and manners, will meet resistance, it is necessary in practice to abolish or lessen sexual differences, at least the important ones. The meaning of gender neutrality, therefore, is transformed to some degree by the effort required to attain it. From a formal, negative, principle abstracting from sexual differences it becomes an actual, positive reformation so as to do away with them. Because there are no gender-neutral human beings, the gender-neutral society cannot simply let nature take its course: take off the pressure to be your sex, one might think, and both sexes will relax, everyone will become gender-neutral. This will not work; pressure in favor of gender neutrality needs to be applied. For some feminists ... the refashioning goes very far; they believe that gender neutrality can be achieved only if women are as sexually free as the most adventurous men.

Women today want to be equal to men, equal in a way that makes them similar to, or virtually the same as, men. They do not want the sort of equality that might result from being superior at home if inferior at work. They have decided that work is better than home. ...

A gender-neutral society, is a society of independent men and women, especially the latter. Although modern women still have some of the ways of traditional women, they behave much more as only men used to behave. The sexual difference is not so much set aside as actually *diminished*. Not only are women behaving more like men, but also men are more welcoming to such women, more *sensitive* toward them, as we say. The sensitive male is above all sensitive to the desire of women to be like men (though also, in lesser degree, to their desire to remain women and to combine this with the main desire). Such a fellow is no longer the Male Chauvinist Pig he was accused of being when this great change got under way. Men have had to curb, if not totally suppress, their sense of superiority to women. And having done this at the behest of women, they have in a way abandoned the contest and acknowledged the artificiality and fragility of their superiority. By their failure to resist they admit that it is easier to live equally. ...

Traditional Male/Female Roles Still Prevail

[From] the standpoint of the complete gender-neutral society, how little has changed. The late feminist political scientist Susan Okin stated the principle of such a society as "a future in which men and women participated in more or less equal numbers in every sphere of life, from infant care to different kinds of paid work to high-level politics." For "high-level politics" and the like, the truth is that men are still in charge. Men have the highest offices, the leading reputations; they make the discoveries, conceive the theories, win the prizes, start the companies, score the touchdowns. Men run things; women follow, accompany, imitate, elaborate, develop. This is not to say that women do not excel, but they seem still to excel as women, in accordance with the traditional stereotype of women and not the new gender-neutral stereotype. Although the line between male and female occupations is much more blurred than it used to be, particularly in the white-collar professions—lawyers and doctors are now 30 percent women, college teachers 43 percent—significant traces of the old ways remain. Legal assistants are 83 percent women; nurses, 93 percent; dental assistants, 98 percent. Pilots are 96 percent men; truck drivers, 95 percent; construction trades, 96 percent; car mechanics, 98 percent. As children grow up, their teachers are 98 percent women in kindergarten, 83 percent in elementary school, 58 percent in high school, and as we saw, 43 percent in college. In business, women excel in small enterprises, in finding a niche for a specialized ambition. They seem to be less interested in becoming numero uno for its own sake. This is not true in every case, to be sure—think of Margaret Thatcher—but it is true on the whole.

In going to work, women have not deserted the home and most of them show a secret liking for housework. They continue to do more than their share of it, that is, more than an equal share. What they have abandoned is not the home but domesticity—the virtues of the home, the justification for staying home. Cheryl Mendelson's large book *Home Comforts* praises the home virtues that produce home comforts. Its title is a rejoinder to promoters of gender neutrality who would describe home comforts as disagreeable "household chores" The book is a subdued but still very manifest claim on behalf of women to rule the household not from the top by making big decisions but from beneath by assuming the right to declare when it is clean. Even more pronounced than women's penchant for nesting is their desire to take loving care of the babies to be reared in the nest. They take nature's pleasure in giving milk, and they generally enjoy greater intimacy with their babies than do men. This applies, [as revealed] in the recent survey, to women assistant professors, a group likely to be loyal in principle to gender neutrality, and it includes among specific tasks changing diapers, which a majority of the women said they actually enjoyed.

To these reservations against gender neutrality, we may add women's hesitancy to condemn manliness. The gender-neutral society, permits, or rather requires, women to be independent, to carry on their own lives without following in the wake of some man. But suppose you have to fight to maintain your independence? Suppose it is not enough to agitate the community, shame the males, and raise everyone's consciousness? With the disaster of September 11, 2001, Americans were sharply reminded that it is sometimes necessary to fight, and that in the business of government, fighting comes before caring. Women were reminded that men can come in handy. The heroes of that day were (apparently) exclusively male—as were the villains. Does this mean that the gender-neutral society is valid only in peacetime? The situation might make some women wish for the disappearance of men, so as not to be subject either to the threat of their aggression or to its remedy. . . .

We are still in transition from the old patriarchal society to the new gender-neutral one, it might be objected, and it will take time to see the change completed. But it's just a matter of time. To this the answer is, we shall see. Right now there remains an obstacle to gender neutrality—manliness—which does not seem easily removable, even in time. Gender neutrality seems at first to disregard sexual differences, but it also wants women to be more independent, more like men. It assumes that what was until recently specific to men is actually common to both sexes. It requires that we guide ourselves by what is common to the sexes, and this is what we are presently trying to do. Everywhere in the media we see portrayed the aggressive female and the sensitive male—Xena the Warrior Princess and [actors] Alan Alda or Warren Beatty (sometimes together). Both roles are difficult to play, but somehow the latter is more so. Women may have trouble in playing the aggressor, they may not be consistent, they may not be as pleasing to men in the new format; but despite the difficulties they can usually manage. Women are more malleable; they are able to do what men do while still maintaining an identity for themselves specifically as women. Yet men reject and resist the expectation that they should abandon their manliness. They do not so much mind sharing their traditional opportunities with whoever can exploit them, and they have shown newfound respect for women who can. But they draw the line at doing what women have left behind.

In sum, a serious discrepancy exists between what men and women, and especially men, believe, or say they believe, and what they are in fact willing to do. Their unofficial desires are not what they should be officially to maintain the gender-neutral society. Democracy as a whole [nineteenth-century French historian Alexis de] Tocqueville tells us, overthrows the legitimacy of unequal privilege much more easily than it establishes a legitimacy of its own, for one equal person does not see why she should obey another. Today it seems generally admitted that gender neutrality is the only legitimate way to live—yet we are not living that way. . . .

Manly Men Are Confident and Commanding

Manliness tends to be insistent and intolerant, and it is truly a threat to the gender-neutral society. Those who want to "deconstruct" or do away with it may be wrong but they are not anxious over nothing. If manliness exists, it is probably a greater threat than these critics believe. For even if manliness is a social construction, it does not follow that it can be done away with, and reconstructed, overnight. Darwinians . . . believe in a kind of social construction of manliness that has taken place gradually over millions of years. Why would it take less time to reverse the construction? Deconstructing manliness to "masculinity" may rob it of virtue but only confirms its power.

I conclude that we must confront manliness. We cannot escape the gender-neutral society, and we cannot ignore the challenge to it. To establish choice we have to clear away the obstacle to choice. So, what is this manliness, today no longer so chauvinistic as it once was but still disdainful and yet perhaps still appreciated? We need a definition—something provisional—from which to begin.

Manliness is still around, and we still find it attractive. To begin the search for a definition . . . , let's consider what we like about manliness. Two things, I would say, for a start: the *confidence* of manly men and their ability to *command*. The confidence of a manly man gives him independence of others. He is not always asking for help or directions or instructions (for it is out of manliness that men do not like to ask for directions when lost). The manly man is in control when control is difficult or contested—in a situation of risk. He knows his job, and he stands fast in that knowledge. If he doesn't really know his job, his confidence is false and he is just boasting. If he knows it but lets himself be pushed around, he's also not really confident; he merely has the basis for confidence. The first case of boasting is a manly excess, the second is a defect of manliness. For some reason manliness includes, or is hospitable to, too much manliness, but it emphatically rejects a person who has too little of it. Perhaps it is because a manly man wants his manliness to be visible. So he is often portrayed in novels, in the movies, or wherever, in exaggeration, even though too much manliness is also a defect and can have disastrous consequences.

The independence of a manly man would keep him from getting involved with other people. He would be aloof, satisfied with himself and none too interested in other people's problems. At the least, he would wait to intervene until he is called upon to do so. But that degree of independence is in tension with the other manly element, the ability to command. The manly man is good at getting things done, and one reason is that he is good at *ordering* people to get them done. In politics and in other public situations, he willingly takes responsibility when others hang back. He not only stands fast but also steps up to do what is required. In private life, in the family, this ability makes him protective of his wife and children because they are weaker. Being protective (as opposed to nurturing) is a manly form of responsibility in private life analogous to getting into politics in public life. In both there is an easy assumption of authority. Manly men take authority for granted—the need for authority in general and their own particular authority. To the extent that all of us recognize the need for authority, whether emergency or everyday, we are attracted to those who seem to radiate authority and thus inspire confidence.

John Wayne is still every American's idea of manliness. That tells you something about the standing of manliness because John Wayne is not of our generation; in fact, he's dead. He is so far from gender-neutral that one's imagination balks at picturing him as him/her. How could his manliness be abstracted from his easy male swagger? His characters are more manly than the frenetic heroes of today's action movies who do not know how to stay quiet. The typical John Wayne movie shows the conflict between manly independence and manly command, as the question is whether he will be trapped into marriage or some other responsible situation (*Stagecoach*) or remain aloof and wild in his independence (*The Searchers*). Manly men are often not hard for women to catch, but they are not easy to corral. So too in politics, the manly one is often disgusted at the irresponsibility and incompetence of those who got themselves into a mess, and he is strongly tempted, like Gary Cooper in *High Noon*, to leave them there where they belong.

We are attracted to the manly man because he imparts some of his confidence to everyone else. With his self-assumed authority he vindicates justice and makes things turn out right or at least enables us to get even. He not only knows what justice requires, but he acts on his knowledge, making and executing the decision that the rest of us trembled even to define. He knows what he is doing, himself, but in a large sense he represents human competence to all of us. He is manly man asserting the worth of man the human being (perhaps this is why, in English and in other languages, male and human being are both called "man"). In asserting his own worth, he makes us feel worthy too. While admiring him, we come to admire ourselves, since we have someone or something to look up to. Admiration is quite different from sympathy or compassion for someone's suffering. Admiration makes you look up to someone in control, compassion makes you look down to someone in distress. As with manliness, we have lost the idea but not the practice of admiration.

Let us not be too sure about manly confidence, for not everyone finds it attractive. Manliness, like suffering, deals with fear. The Greek word for manliness, *andreia*, is also the word the Greeks used for courage, the virtue concerned with controlling fear. When we come to fear, we enter the dark side of manliness. Manly men rise above their fear, but in doing so they carry, their fear with them, though it is under control. Some say that manly men do not truly control their fear; they continue to struggle with it. The struggling takes the form of boasting they can overcome fear. But can they? In this view, manliness is based on the anxiety, of losing one's manliness. Manly men are not confident but actually fearful. When they try to command, they become bullies. In our century, these critics say, we have seen the epitome of manliness in fascism, the theory and practice of loud, boastful, bullying, swaggering—and murderous—men. . . .

The Nobility of Manliness

So we are beginning to get a picture of manliness, neither altogether favorable nor repellent. Manliness can have something heroic about it. . . .

It lives for action, yet is also boastful about what manly men will do and have done. It jeers at those who do not seem manly and asks us continually to prove ourselves. It defines turf and fights for it, sometimes for no good reason, sometimes to defend precious rights. And it exaggerates its independence, as if action were an end in itself and manly men were the best or only kind of human being.

This is only the beginning of a definition, but it is solid enough from which to see that manliness is both good and bad. Manliness has always been attractive, but equally it has always lived under a cloud of doubt. The doubt is raised perhaps by men who do not have the time or taste for manliness. This suggests that it is possible that manliness is not in the interest of men, or of all men, let alone women.

What prevents a woman from being manly? Today we must explain what has for so long, for millennia, been taken for granted. Are not women as confident as men? They are in their way. A lady has been defined as one who never loses her dignity regardless of the situation. But this virtue does not encourage her, may even prevent her, from seeking out situations of risk in which her dignity is challenged. . . .

Manliness is knowing how to be confident in situations where sufficient knowledge is not available.

Most people are either too enthusiastic about manliness or too dismissive of it. They think that manliness is the only virtue, and all virtue; or they think it is the last, stupid stereotype, soon to be dead as a dodo. To study it well, the trick is not to get carried away to either extreme. Yet manliness is a passionate quality, and it often leads to getting carried away, whether for good or ill. A sober, scholarly treatment risks failing to convey the nobility of manliness—it's so easy to make fun of. That's particularly true today when the picture of manliness conveyed to us is as direct and unsubtle as the actor Russell Crowe in *Gladiator*, the singer Ted Nugent in *Cat Scratch Fever*, and the wrestler Jesse Ventura in *Governor of Minnesota*.

So, we are confronted with a manliness that in refusing an equal share of housework disdains women as such, irrationally and indiscriminately—stereotypically. A manliness, too, that seeks glory in risk and cannot abide the rational life of peace and security. And a manliness that yearns for deference from the women it looks down on. In the book of an educated woman I came across this piece of wisdom quoted from another woman, not deeply educated: "The problem is that men need to feel important." Exactly!

A New Gender Divide

Kathleen Gerson

Kathleen Gerson finds that while today's young adults enjoy numerous options, they still struggle with decisions about marriage, children, and careers. Grappling with their own family experiences has led most young men and women to affirm the intrinsic importance of a traditional family, but also to seek ways to blend a committed relationship with a substantial measure of independence. Since a mother's earnings and a father's involvement are both integral to the economic and emotional welfare of children, Gerson asserts that more flexible workplaces are needed. The best family values will emerge, she points out, only if we as a society provide social supports to allow young people to overcome work/family conflicts. Gerson is a professor of sociology at New York University and president-elect of the Eastern Sociological Society. She is the author of several books on sociology and is completing a new book, The Children of the Gender Revolution.

Young workers today grew up in rapidly changing times: They watched women march into the workplace and adults develop a wide range of alternatives to traditional marriage. Now making their own passage to adulthood, these "children of the gender revolution" have inherited a far different world from that of their parents or grandparents. They may enjoy an expanded set of options, but they also face rising uncertainty about whether and how to craft a marriage, rear children, and build a career.

Considering the scope of these new uncertainties, it is understandable that social forecasters are pondering starkly dif-

Kathleen Gerson, "What Do Women and Men Want? Many of the Same Things—but Our System Contributes to Gender Conflicts over Work, Parenting, and Marriage," *The American Prospect*, vol. 18, no. 3, March 2007, pp. A8–A11.

ferent possibilities for the future. Focusing on a comparatively small recent upturn in the proportion of mothers who do not hold paid jobs, some are pointing to a "return to tradition," especially among young women. Others see evidence of a "decline of commitment" in the rising number of young adults who are living outside a married relationship. However, the 120 in-depth interviews I conducted between 1998 and 2003 with young adults from diverse backgrounds make it clear that neither of these scenarios does justice to the lessons gleaned from growing up in changing families or to the strategies being crafted in response to deepening work/family dilemmas.

Keenly aware of the obstacles to integrating work and family life in an egalitarian way, most young adults are formulating a complicated set of ideals and fallback positions. Women and men largely share similar aspirations: Most wish to forge a lifelong partnership that combines committed work with devoted parenting. These ideals are tempered, however, by deep and realistic fears that rigid, time-demanding jobs and a dearth of child-care or family-leave options block the path to such a goal. Confronted with so many obstacles, young women and men today are pursuing fallback strategies as insurance in the all-too-likely event that their egalitarian ideals prove out of reach.

These second-best strategies are not only different but also at odds with each other. If a supportive, egalitarian partnership is not possible, most women prefer individual autonomy over becoming dependent on a husband in a traditional marriage. Most men, however, if they can't have an equal balance between work and parenting, fall back on a neotraditional arrangement that allows them to put their own work prospects first and rely on a partner for most caregiving. The best hope for bridging this new gender divide lies in creating social policies that would allow new generations to create the families they want rather than the families they believe they must settle for.

Growing Up in Changing Families

In contrast to the conventional wisdom that children are best reared in families with a homemaking mother and bread-winning father, the women and men who grew up in such circumstances hold divided assessments. While a little more than half thought this was the best arrangement, a little less than half thought otherwise. When domesticity appeared to undermine their mother's satisfaction, disturb the household's harmony, or threaten its economic security, the adult children surveyed concluded that it would have been better if their mothers had pursued a sustained commitment to work or, in some instances, if their parents had separated.

Many of those who grew up in a single-parent home also express ambivalence. Slightly more than half wished their parents had stayed together, but close to half believed that a breakup, while not ideal, was better than continuing to live in a conflict-ridden home or with a neglectful or abusive parent. The longer-term consequences of a breakup had a crucial influence on the lessons children drew. The children whose parents got back on their feet and created better lives developed surprisingly positive outlooks on the decision to separate.

Those who grew up in dual-earner homes were least ambivalent about their parents' arrangements. More than three-fourths thought their parents had chosen the best option. Having two work-committed parents not only provided increased economic resources for the family but also promoted marriages that seemed more egalitarian and satisfying. Yet when the pressures of parents working long hours or coping with blocked opportunities and family-unfriendly workplaces took their toll, some children came to believe that having overburdened, time-stressed caretakers offset the advantages of living in a two-income household.

In short, the generation that grew up in this era of changing families is more focused on how well parents (and other caretakers) were able to meet the twin challenges of providing economic and emotional support rather than on what forms households took. Children were more likely to receive that support when their parents (or other guardians) could find secure and personally satisfying jobs, high-quality child care, and a supportive partnership that left room for a measure of personal autonomy.

New Ideals, Persisting Barriers

So what do young adults want for themselves? Grappling with their own family experiences has led most young women and men to affirm the intrinsic importance of family life, but also to search for ways to combine lasting commitment with a substantial measure of independence. Whether or not their parents stayed together, the overwhelming majority of young adults I interviewed said they hope to rear their children in the context of a lifelong intimate bond. They have certainly not given up on the value or possibility of commitment. It would be a mistake, however, to equate this ideal with a desire to be in a traditional relationship. While almost everyone wants to create a lasting marriage—or, in the case of same-sex couples, a "marriage-like" relationship—most also want to find an egalitarian partnership with considerable room for personal autonomy. Not surprisingly, three-fourths of those who grew up in dual-earner homes want their spouses to share breadwinning and caretaking; but so do more than two-thirds of those from more traditional homes, and close to nine-tenths of those with single parents. Four-fifths of women want egalitarian relationships, but so do two-thirds of the men. Whether reared by traditional, dual-earning, or single parents, the overwhelming majority of women and men want a committed bond where both paid work and family caretaking are shared.

Amy, an Asian American with two working parents, and Michael, an African American raised by a single mother, express essentially the same hopes:

Amy: I want a 50-50 relationship, where we both have the potential of doing everything—both of us working and dealing with kids. With regard to career, if neither has flexibility, then one of us will have to sacrifice for one period, and the other for another.

Michael: I don't want the '50s type of marriage, where I come home and she's cooking. She doesn't have to cook; I like to cook. I want her to have a career of her own. I want to be able to set my goals, and she can do what she wants, too, because we both have this economic base and the attitude to do it. That's what marriage is about.

Young adults today are affirming the value of commitment while also challenging traditional forms of marriage. Women and men both want to balance family and work in their own lives and balance commitment and autonomy in their relationships. Yet women and men also share a concern that—in the face of workplaces greedy for time and communities lacking adequate child care—insurmountable obstacles block the path to achieving these goals.

Chris, a young man of mixed ancestry whose parents shared work and caretaking, thus wonders: "I thought you could just have a relationship—that love and being happy was all that was needed in life—but I've learned it's a difficult thing. So that would be my fear: Where am I cutting into my job too much? Where am I cutting into the relationship too much? How do I divide it? And can it be done at all? Can you blend these two parts of your world?"

A New Gender Divide

The rising conflicts between family and work make equal sharing seem elusive and possibly unattainable. Most young adults have concluded that they have little choice but to prepare for options that are likely to fall substantially short of their ideals. In the face of these barriers, women and men are formulating different—and opposing—fallback strategies.

A "traditional" family, in which the male is the main breadwinner and the female does most of the childrearing, is not always the only choice for today's parents. Laura Bowen and her husband Dave Shelly, seen here, work as computer game designers and alternate childcare duties based on who has the busier work schedule. © Bob Sacha/Corbis.

In contrast to the media-driven message that more women are opting for domestic pursuits, the vast majority of women I interviewed say they are determined to seek financial and emotional self-reliance, even at the expense of a committed relationship. Most young women—regardless of class, race, or ethnicity—are reluctant to surrender their autonomy in a traditional marriage. When the bonds of marriage are so fragile, relying on a husband for economic security seems foolhardy. And if a relationship deteriorates, economic dependence on a man leaves few means of escape.

Danisha, an African American who grew up in an inner-city, working-class neighborhood, and Jennifer, who was raised in a middle-class, predominantly white suburb, agree:

> Danisha: Let's say that my marriage doesn't work. Just in case, I want to establish myself, because I don't ever want to end up, like, "What am I going to do?" I want to be able to do what I have to do and still be OK.

Jennifer: I will have to have a job and some kind of stability before considering marriage. Too many of my mother's friends went for that—"Let him provide everything"—and they're stuck in a very unhappy relationship, but can't leave because they can't provide for themselves or the children they now have. So it's either welfare or putting up with somebody else's trap.

Hoping to avoid being trapped in an unhappy marriage or abandoned by an unreliable partner, almost three-fourths of women surveyed said they plan to build a non-negotiable base of self-reliance and an independent identity in the world of paid work. But they do not view this strategy as incompatible with the search for a life partner. Instead, it reflects their determination to set a high standard for a worthy relationship. Economic self-reliance and personal independence make it possible to resist "settling" for anything less than a satisfying, mutually supportive bond.

Maria, who grew up in a two-parent home in a predominantly white, working-class suburb and Rachel, whose Latino parents separated when she was young, share this view:

Maria: I want to have this person to share [my] life with—[someone] that you're there for as much as they're there for you. But I can't settle.

Rachel: I'm not afraid of being alone, but I am afraid of being with somebody who's a jerk. I want to get married and have children, but it has to be under the right circumstances, with the right person.

Maria and Rachel also agree that if a worthy relationship ultimately proves out of reach, then remaining single need not mean social disconnection. Kin and friends provide a support network that enlarges and, if needed, even substitutes for an intimate relationship:

Maria: If I don't find [a relationship], then I cannot live in sorrow. It's not the only thing that's ultimately important. If

I didn't have my family, if I didn't have a career, if I didn't have friends, I would be equally unhappy. [A relationship] is just one slice of the pie.

Rachel: I can spend the rest of my life on my own, and as long as I have my sisters and my friends, I'm OK.

By blending support from friends and kin with financial self-sufficiency, most young women are pursuing a strategy of autonomy rather than placing their own fate or their children's in the hands of a traditional marriage. Whether or not this strategy ultimately leads to marriage, it appears to offer the safest and most responsible way to prepare for the uncertainties of relationships and the barriers to men's equal sharing.

It Is Different for Men

Young men, in contrast, face a different dilemma: Torn between women's pressures for an egalitarian partnership and their own desire to succeed—or at least survive—in time-demanding workplaces, they are more inclined to fall back on a modified traditionalism that recognizes a mother's right (and need) to work but puts a man's claim to a career first.

Despite growing up in a two-income home, Andrew distinguishes between a woman's "choice" to work and a man's "responsibility" to support his family: "I would like to have it be equal—just from what I was exposed to and what attracts me—but I don't have a set definition for what that would be like. I would be fine if both of us were working, but if she thought, 'At this point in my life, I don't want to work,' then it would be fine."

This model makes room for two earners, but it positions men as the breadwinning specialists. When push comes to shove, and the demands of work collide with the needs of children, this framework allows fathers to resist equal caretaking, even in a two-earner context. Although Josh's mother became too mentally ill to care for her children or herself, Josh plans to leave the lion's share of caretaking to his wife:

All things being equal, it [caretaking] should be shared. It may sound sexist, but if somebody's going to be the breadwinner, it's going to be me. First of all, I make a better salary, and I feel the need to work, and I just think the child really needs the mother more than the father at a young age.

Men are thus more likely to favor a fallback arrangement that retains the gender boundary between breadwinning and caretaking, even when mothers hold paid jobs. From young men's perspective, this modified but still gendered household offers women the chance to earn income and establish an identity at the workplace without imposing the costs of equal parenting on men. Granting a mother's "right" to work supports women's claims for independence, but does not undermine men's claim that their work prospects should come first. Acknowledging men's responsibilities at home provides for more involved fatherhood, but does not envision domestic equality. And making room for two earners provides a buffer against the difficulties of living on one income, but does not challenge men's position as the primary earner. Modified traditionalism thus appears to be a good compromise when the career costs of equality remain so high. Ultimately, however, men's desire to protect work prerogatives collides with women's growing demand for equality and independence.

Getting Past the Work/Family Impasse

If the realities of time-demanding workplaces and missing supports for caregiving make it difficult for young adults to achieve the sharing, flexible, and more egalitarian relationships most want, then how can we get past this impasse? Clearly, most young women are not likely to answer this question by returning to patterns that fail to speak to either their highest ideals or their greatest fears. To the contrary, they are forming fallback strategies that stress personal autonomy, including the possibility of single parenthood. Men's most common responses to economic pressures and time-demanding jobs stress a different strategy—one that allows for two incomes but preserves men's claim on the most rewarding careers. Women and men are leaning in different directions, and their conflicting responses are fueling a new gender divide. But this schism stems from the intensification of long-simmering work/family dilemmas, not from a decline of laudable values.

We need to worry less about the family values of a new generation and more about the institutional barriers that make them so difficult to achieve. Most young adults do not wish to turn back the clock, but they do hope to combine the more traditional value of making a lifelong commitment with the more modern value of having a flexible, egalitarian relationship. Rather than trying to change individual values, we need to provide the social supports that will allow young people to overcome work/family conflicts and realize their most cherished aspirations.

Since a mother's earnings and a father's involvement are both integral to the economic and emotional welfare of children (and also desired by most women and men), we can achieve the best family values only by creating flexible workplaces, ensuring equal economic opportunity for women, outlawing discrimination against all parents, and building child-friendly communities with plentiful, affordable, and high-quality child care. These long overdue policies will help new generations create the more egalitarian partnerships they desire. Failure to build institutional supports for new social realities will not produce a return to traditional marriage. Instead, following the law of unintended consequences, it will undermine marriage itself.

For Further Discussion

1. In Chapter 1, James Nagel writes that Hemingway's "personal life has become so involved with his work that the two are virtually inseparable in scholarly inquiry." Hemingway used events and people from his life to form the basis of *The Sun Also Rises*. Do you think that Jake Barnes is speaking for Hemingway in the novel and thus is a reliable narrator? Why or why not?

2. Early in the novel, Jake says to Robert Cohn, "Nobody ever lives their life all the way up except bullfighters." In Chapter 2, Sibbie O'Sullivan says that Brett and Jake's relationship, along with the bullfights, are the only things of permanence in the novel. What role does bullfighting play in the novel? What are some of the male-male relationships in the novel and how do they contrast with the male-female relationships?

3. Lady Brett Ashley is interpreted differently by different critics. In Chapter 2, Edmund Wilson, Leslie Fiedler, and Carlos Baker view her as a neurotic bitch, while Lorie Watkins Fulton and Sibbie O'Sullivan find her a positive force and a woman fully worthy of Jake's devotion, and Wendy Martin and Sam Baskett consider her a complex character, with both positive and negative characteristics. From your reading of *The Sun Also Rises*, which critics do you agree with? Cite evidence from the text of *The Sun Also Rises* to support your position.

4. At the end of *The Sun Also Rises*, Brett says, "we could have had such a damned good time together," to which Jake replies, "Isn't it pretty to think so?" In Chapter 2, Lorie Watkins Fulton suggests this is a positive ending, as it means the two can have a friendship, which is likelier

to be longer lasting than a sexual union. In Chapter 1, James Nagel sees little optimism in the ending, suggesting the "novel ends where it began, with Brett and Jake trapped in a hopeless love for each other." Do you agree with either critic, and if so, why? Or do you have a different interpretation for the ending?

5. In Chapter 3, Peter Hyman, Stephen J. Ducat, and Harvey C. Mansfield present three very different perspectives on contemporary manliness. Contrast their views of the contemporary male role to the Hemingway code hero as described by Arnold E. Davidson and Cathy N. Davidson in Chapter 2.

For Further Reading

Paul Bowles   *The Sheltering Sky*. New York: New Directions, 1949.

F. Scott Fitzgerald   *The Great Gatsby*. New York: Scribner's, 1925.

F. Scott Fitzgerald   *Tender Is the Night*. New York: Scribner's, 1934.

F. Scott Fitzgerald   *This Side of Paradise*. New York: Scribner's, 1920.

Ford Madox Ford   *The Good Soldier: A Tale of Passion*. London: John Lane, 1915.

Ford Madox Ford   *Parade's End*. New York: Knopf, 1950.

Graham Greene   *The End of the Affair*. New York: Viking, 1951.

John Hawkes   *The Blood Oranges*. New York: New Directions, 1971.

Ernest Hemingway   *A Farewell to Arms*. New York: Scribner's, 1929.

Ernest Hemingway   *For Whom the Bell Tolls*. New York: Scribner's, 1940.

Ernest Hemingway   *The Garden of Eden*. New York: Scribner's, 1986.

Ernest Hemingway   *A Moveable Feast*. New York: Scribner's, 1964.

Anthony Powell	"A Dance to the Music of Time" series. 12 vols. Various publishers, 1951–76. Omnibus vols. Boston: Little, Brown, 1963–76.
Erich Maria Remarque	*All Quiet on the Western Front.* Boston: Little, Brown, 1929.
Erich Maria Remarque	*Three Comrades.* Boston: Little, Brown, 1937.

Bibliography

Books

John W. Crowley   *The White Logic: Alcoholism and Gender in American Modern Fiction.* Amherst: University of Massachusetts Press, 1994.

Scott Donaldson, ed.   *The Cambridge Companion to Hemingway.* Cambridge, UK: Cambridge University Press, 1996.

Carl P. Eby   *Hemingway's Fetishism: Psychoanalysis and the Mirror of Manhood.* SUNY Series in Psychoanalysis. Albany: State University of New York Press, 1999.

Robert W. Lewis Jr.   *Hemingway on Love.* Austin: University of Texas Press, 1965.

Debra A. Moddelmog   *Reading Desire: In Pursuit of Ernest Hemingway.* Ithaca, NY: Cornell University Press, 1999.

James Nagel, ed.   *Ernest Hemingway: The Writer in Context.* Madison: University of Wisconsin Press, 1984.

James Nagel, ed.   *Critical Essays on Ernest Hemingway's "The Sun Also Rises."* New York: G.K. Hall, 1995.

Earl Rovit   *Ernest Hemingway.* New York: Twayne, 1963.

Mark Spilka   *Hemingway's Quarrel with Androgyny.*
Lincoln: University of Nebraska
Press, 1990.

Thomas Strychacz   *Hemingway's Theatres of Masculinity.*
Baton Rouge: Louisiana State Univer-
sity Press, 2003.

Shira Tarrant   *When Sex Becomes Gender.* Perspectives on Gender. New York: Rout-
ledge, 2006.

Roger Whitlow   *Cassandra's Daughters: The Women in
Hemingway.* Contributions in
Women's Studies. Westport, CT:
Greenwood, 1984.

Delbert F. Wylder   *Hemingway's Heroes.* Albuquerque:
University of New Mexico Press,
1969.

Philip Young   *Ernest Hemingway: A Reconsideration.*
University Park: Pennsylvania State
University Press, 1966.

Periodicals

David Blackmore   "'In New York It'd Mean I
Was a . . .': Masculine Anxiety
and Period Discourses of Sexuality
in *The Sun Also Rises,*" *Hemingway
Review,* vol. 18, no. 1, fall 1988.

Milton A. Cohen   "Circe and Her Swine: Domination
and Debasement in *The Sun Also
Rises,*" *Arizona Quarterly: A Journal of
American Literature, Culture, and
Theory,* vol. 41, no. 4, winter 1985.

Robert D. Crozier "The Mask of Death, the Face of Life: Hemingway's Feminique," *The Hemingway Review*, vol. 8, no. 1, 1984.

Loretta Dickey "Intergendering: Resolving the Duality of Gender," *off our backs*, vol. 34, nos. 9–10, September–October 2004.

Ira Elliott "Performance Art: Jake Barnes and 'Masculine' Signification in *The Sun Also Rises*," *American Literature*, vol. 67, no. 1, March 1995.

Greg Forter "Melancholy Modernism: Gender and the Politics of Mourning in *The Sun Also Rises*," *Hemingway Review*, vol. 21, no. 1, fall 2001.

Linda R. Hirshman "Homeward Bound: 'Choice Feminism' Claims That Staying Home with the Kids Is Just One More Feminist Choice. Funny That Most Men Rarely Make the Same 'Choice.' Exactly What Kind of Choice Is That?" *The American Prospect*, vol. 16, no. 12, December 2005.

Gerald Kennedy "Hemingway's Gender Trouble," *American Literature*, vol. 63, 1991.

Sukrita Paul Kumar "Woman as Hero in Hemingway's *The Sun Also Rises*," *The Literary Endeavor*, vol. 6, nos. 1–4, 1985.

Jacob Michael
Leland

"Yes, That Is a Roll of Bills in My Pocket: The Economy of Masculinity in *The Sun Also Rises*," *Hemingway Review*, vol. 23, no. 2, spring 2004.

Todd Onderdonk

"'Bitched': Feminization, Identity, and the Hemingwayesque in *The Sun Also Rises*," *Twentieth-Century Literature*, vol. 52, no. 1, spring 2006.

Wolfgang E.H.
Rudat

"Sexual Dilemmas in *The Sun Also Rises*: Hemingway's Count and the Education of Jacob Barnes," *The Hemingway Review*, vol. 8, no. 2, spring 1989.

Jenn Ruddy

"Men, Masculinity and Feminism." *Briarpatch*, vol. 35, no. 2, March–April 2006.

Elizabeth A. Suter
and Paige W.
Toller

"Gender Roles and Feminism Revisited: A Follow Up Study," *Sex Roles*, vol. 55, nos. 1–2, July 2006.

Delbert E. Wylder

"The Two Faces of Brett: The Role of the New Woman in *The Sun Also Rises*," *Kentucky Philological Review*, 1980, pp. 27–33.

Index

Men
aspirations of, 194, 196–197
earthly paradise for, 95–96
feminine side of, 151–157
friendships between, 137–139
ideal, 98–99
impact of WWI on, 11–12
manly, 180–192
pressures on today's, 200–201
without women, 91–92
working-class, 160–161
Men Without Women
(Hemingway), 25–26
Mendelson, cheryl, 186
Metrosexuals, 151–157
Mike Campbell (character), 49, 57,
82–83, 105
Moddelmog, Debra A., 141
Modern woman. *See* New Woman
Modern world, contradictions of,
101
Money
as metaphor, 104–105, 112–
113
sex and, 103
Montana, 96
Moral characters, 50–53
Morality
Jake and, 123–124
money and, 104–105
mothers and, 109–110
pragmatic, 36
Mother role, 109–110
A Moveable Feast (Hemingway),
29, 34
"My Old Man" (Hemingway), 24
Mythological methods, 53–55

N

Nagel, James, 22
Narrative style, 24, 30
Negation, 71

Neurotic characters, 49, 137–138
New Woman
Brett as, 79–82, 97–107
fashions of, 100–101
qualities of, 12, 99–100
Nick Adams (character), 32–33,
39, 89
Nihilism, 39–40
Nobel Prize, 29

O

Observation, 73–74
Okin, Susan, 185
The Old Man and the Sea
(Hemingway), 28–29, 33
Openness, 139–140
O'Sullivan, Sibbie, 129
In Our Time (Hemingway), 25
"Out of Season" (Hemingway),
24–25

P

Paganism, 54–55, 58, 82, 95
Panic, 40
Parallelism, 35
Paris, 24, 30–31
Passion, 106
Passos, John Dos, 10
Pedro Romero (character)
Brett and, 31–32, 85–87, 113,
122–123, 138, 144, 147–148
Jake and, 146, 147–148
masculinity of, 57–58, 66–67
as moral character, 49, 50–53
performance of, 73–77
sexual imagery and, 64–67
as symbol of masculine cour-
age, 106
Performance, 72–78, 86
Perkins, Maxwell, 49, 52